AN ARTIST'S BOOK OF INSPIRATION

AN ARTIST'S BOOK OF INSPIRATION

A Collection of Thoughts on Art, Artists, and Creativity

Compiled and Edited by
ASTRID FITZGERALD

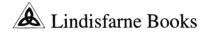 Lindisfarne Books

Published in the United States by Lindisfarne Books

Library of Congress Cataloging-in-Publication Data

An artist's book of inspiration : a collection of thougts on art,
artists, and creativity / compiled and edited by Astrid Fitzgerald.
    p. cm.
Includes bibliographical references and index.
ISBN 0-940262-76-2 (paper)
1. Art—Quotations, maxims, etc. 2. Artists—Quotations,
maxims, etc. 3. Creation (Literary, artistic, etc.)—Quotations,
maxims, etc. I. Fitzgerald, Astrid, 1938–
PN6084.A8A77 1996
700—dc20   96-20780
                                                          CIP

Cover art: Astrid Fitzgerald

Cover design: Whitehouse & Company
Book design: Watersign Resources

For Kent

In the course of my life I have often had the same dream, appearing in different forms at different times, but always saying the same thing: "Socrates, practice and cultivate the arts."

—**Plato**, *Phaedo*

I wish to thank all my teachers for their patience and wisdom, my friends and fellow artists for their help and encouragement, and Mary Ellen Doyle for helping in the selection of the art-work. Special thanks to my husband, the writer Richard Gel-dard, for his constant support and editorial assistance, particularly in ordering the material and titling the quota-tions. I also thank Christopher Bamford of Lindisfarne Press for his faith in this project. I am grateful to all men and women who have lived "the examined life," have shared their insights into the mystery of life, and have given expression to their wonder and delight through music, words, and the visual arts.

CONTENTS

PREFACE   xi

PART I   *The Ground of Artistic Being*
            ULTIMATE SOURCES   2
            ETERNAL LIGHT   6
            UNITY   7

PART II   *The Field of Creative Play*
            COSMOS   12
            NATURE   14
            CULTURE   19

PART III   *The Universal Qualities and Forces
            of Creativity*
            SOUL   26
            LOVE   30
            BEAUTY   33

PART IV   *The Flowering of Creative Energy*
            CONCEPTION   42
            FORCES   48
            STATES   52
            ACTION   58

Contents

PART V   *The Faculties of Creative Expression*

CONSCIOUSNESS   64

ASPECTS OF MIND   68

EMOTION   74

SENSES   78

PART VI   *The Nature of the Calling*

IDEALS   84

PASSION   92

SELF-DISCOVERY   96

OBEDIENCE   100

A UNIQUE VOICE   102

SERVE THE WORLD   106

PART VII   *The Ideals of Artistic Expression*

SOURCES   110

HIGHEST IDEALS   112

UNIVERSAL PRINCIPLES   117

ELEVATING THE HUMAN SPIRIT   126

TRANSFORMING LIFE AND SOCIETY   131

PART VIII   *Infinite Forms of Expression*

IDEALS   140

MODES   144

MEANS   150

ARTICULATION   152

PART IX   *The Dynamics of Creative Work*

GATHERING FORCES   158

CREATIVE EFFORT   161

STATES OF MIND   168

BEYOND DOING 175

ATTENTION 178

MEASURE 180

METHOD 182

STRUGGLE 186

PART X *The Experience of the Creative Life*

DAY-TO-DAY 194

RECOGNITION 202

STEPPING BACK 207

PERSEVERANCE 211

BALANCE 215

DEVOTION 217

ACKNOWLEDGMENTS 221

BIBLIOGRAPHY 224

ADDITIONAL SOURCES 233

INDEX OF AUTHORS 234

ARTWORK CREDITS 238

PREFACE

Creative expression, invention, and the need to do a thing well are fundamental to human life. When in these pursuits we aspire to their highest goal, we indeed find our highest calling. Art, in its myriad forms, ennobles the maker and has the power to transform the beholder and, at times, society. Great architecture raises our consciousness, music vibrates in our hearts and minds, and dance delights and uplifts. We know with certainty that art is a necessity, that we come closest to God when we become creators. We also know that without art, we become dehumanized.

Artists, writers, and philosophers have defined art and its role for over two thousand years. The great ideas on art and expressions of the creative process contained in this volume have at one time or another inspired me in my own quest for self-expression through painting. These words of wisdom have nourished my ground of being, have strengthened my reason and intellect, and have given me courage in times of struggle and doubt.

Some of these quotations from my notebooks have the weight of aphorisms — they sing with the certainty of the sage. Others are idealistic, some even romantic; some may be tinged with the opinions of the age. But they all have to me the ring of truth, and some have the power to reverberate in the heart and fire the intuition and creativity. It is my hope that they do not merely add to the storehouse of opinion, of which we certainly have too much — and that they do not indicate a predilection for any one particular form of expression.

Rather, the artist and the art-lover are urged to listen to the wisdom of the ages, to go back to the sources of the inquiries and seek answers to the fundamental questions: What am I? What is nature? What is life? What is art? From this introspection a new world view may arise, beliefs and values may be challenged, and the constructs of our own reality may be called into question.

Art constantly seeks to redefine itself, to find new and original modes of expression. But have we sometimes sacrificed meaning and essence on the altar of the innovative, the outrageous, and the politically correct? Should we be concerned when the language — the "artspeak" used to describe the "isms," "posts," and "neos"— has to be constantly explained and redefined, and even then can barely keep up with the shifts in style and form?

We live in a postmodern era devoid of artistic standards. The movements of the last thirty years have successfully demystified art and the making of art. The role of art has not been clearly defined in recent times, and artists and students of art rarely gather to examine and discuss the calling to creative work. The artistic process is a dizzying ride, with frequently shifting gears and no sense of direction. When human beings have been reduced by modernism to biological machinery or psychological determinism, artists are left with a much narrowed field of exploration. Thus, the creative output presents us with images of fear, madness, despair, and decadence. The art of our time seems to be self-destructive, broadening the gap between audience and the creative output. The eye of the artist has turned to the exterior, to the biennials and the market place, seeking direction, and thus we have art that moves further and further away from our inner nature. As a result, we have art that is based on concept instead of idea and inspiration, art that ends up commenting on itself or upon the absence of values.

Wassily Kandinsky sought to free art from outmoded forms and to find a new but universal language based on what he termed the "inner need" of the artist. His book, Concerning the Spiritual in Art, *published in 1911, gives voice to his vision. It is a deep philosophical exploration expressed with such purity of thought that it remains to this day a source of inspiration. He clearly saw the heights to which art and artist can attain. Even today, serious men and women are creating art that aspires to these high ideals. These works by quiet, devoted creators do not meet with the current trends and unfortunately seldom find their way into the public view. I dare to think that there is a stream of art of the spirit, which will be acknowledged as soon as we invent a new forum to make it accessible to those who share the same vision.*

PREFACE

Artists have a great responsibility in what they bring into the world. They have to take great care which ideas they choose to express, to which feelings and emotions they give form. There are some indications that "life imitates art" and not the other way around, suggesting that artists have the power to create a new reality and thus must discern very carefully what they set into motion.

There are times when artists have to go backstage, as it were, to change costume, to rest, to reflect, and to gather spiritual and emotional strength for the next entrance. This process sometimes takes place spontaneously: it comes in the form of a dry period. At other times the need to rethink is a conscious decision and comes at the height of a career, when the work contains all that wants to be said in the most skillful way possible — when it all comes together in a beautiful synthesis. The artist may feel the need to throw it all out, rather than be repetitive, and to let go of a hard-won repository of techniques, skills, and modes. This withdrawal is no small thing and takes great courage and integrity. The fear of "losing the edge," of never working again can be very frightening. There is a sense of doubt and loss when long-cherished ideas, sketches, and plans are abandoned. When this letting go is complete, a vacuum is created and pulls in fresh air and new ideas. From this introspection comes a new order, an influx of a finer energy — the substance necessary and conducive to creativity.

It is by withdrawing, renewing, tending to the ground of being that an artist can give to the world what in ordinary life is lacking: peace, order, beauty — a reflection of our true nature, an opening into the world beyond manifestation. Through introspection the artist's inner world grows, the field expands, and wisdom finds expression in an iconography that is personal and yet universal and intelligible. By following "his bliss," the artist finally serves the world. As Emerson put it, "By doing his work he makes the need felt which he can supply, and creates the taste by which he is enjoyed."

The quotations in this book are offered to the reader in the spirit of exploration: Consider this! Reflect on that! See what arises in your mind! When the ideas expressed contradict your own beliefs, the tension produced may elicit your own truth and challenge you to formulate what it is you believe. Some of the quotations are in direct opposition to contemporary values. The friction of disagreement may challenge you to further consideration and discourse.

It is my hope that some of the inspirational expressions reveal some truth, sound a note that resonates in your innermost being. The ideas expressed may provide a touchstone for your creative forces, a new place to stand with courage and conviction from which a renewed creative impulse will spring forth.

This selection from my notebooks is offered with love and compassion to all those who are compelled to create and give of themselves to the world and all those who hunger for an art of the spirit.

— Astrid Fitzgerald

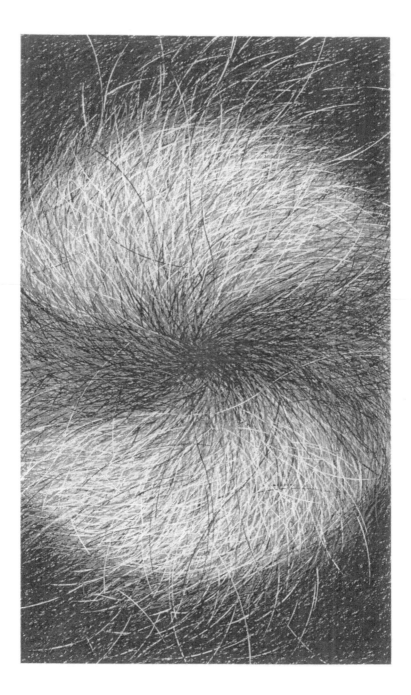

PART I

The Ground of
Artistic Being

*T*he ground of my being is not a place, is not a substance, but
an infinite field of potentiality — a vast ocean of consciousness. All movement begins in this potentiality and becomes
desire, thought, and action.

When the burden of "doing" becomes oppressive and the con-
cerns of creative work deteriorate into the "how," I experience a
sense of loss — a loss of essence — of memory of my true
nature. At such times I look to the wisdom of the great philosophers, I listen to the music of Mozart, Bach, or Beethoven. I am
reminded of the eternally unchanging. I sit and wait. I become
still. I realize that I am not this form, that I am not the intellect. I remember. I enjoy that pure feeling of existence that I have
known in moments of grace since childhood. In this state there is
no desire, no searching; I am home. But not for long. Too soon, I
become conscious again of time and place, and the forces of
nature will have me think and act and co-create the world
anew, holding fast to the great illusion.

1

The undying blazing spirit

Shining, yet hidden, Spirit lives in the cavern. Everything that sways, breathes, opens, closes, lives in Spirit; beyond learning, beyond everything, better than anything; living, unliving.

It is the undying blazing Spirit, that seed of all seeds, wherein lay hidden the world and all its creatures. It is life, speech, mind, reality, immortality. It is there to be struck. Strike it, my son!

— Mundaka-Upanishad

Universal Being

Standing on the bare ground, —my head bathed by the blithe air, and uplifted into infinite space, —all mean egotism vanishes. I become a transparent eyeball, I am nothing. I see all. The currents of the Universal Being circulate through me; I am part or particle of God.

— Ralph Waldo Emerson

The Great Self

Beyond the senses there are the objects, beyond the objects there is the mind, beyond the mind there is the intellect, the Great Self is beyond the intellect.

Beyond the Great there is the Undeveloped, beyond the Undeveloped there is the person (*purusha*). Beyond the person there is nothing — this is the goal, the highest road.

— Upanishads

Ultimate Sources

Eye on the eternal

Whenever, therefore, the maker of anything keeps his eye on the eternally unchanging and uses it as his pattern for the form and function of his product the result must be good; whenever he looks to something that has come to be and uses a model that has come to be, the result is not good . . . .

If the world is beautiful and its maker good, clearly he had his eye on the eternal; if the alternative (which it is blasphemy even to mention) is true, on that which is subject to change. Clearly, of course, he had his eye on the eternal; for the world is the fairest of all things that have come into being and he is the best of causes.

— Plato

Tao as source of divinity

Tao has reality and substance, but no action or form. It can be given but not received. It is attainable but invisible. It is its own source and its own root. It existed before heaven and earth and for all eternity. It causes spirits and gods to be divine. It begets heaven and earth. It is above the zenith and yet not high. It is below the nadir and yet not low. It was born before heaven and earth but not long ago. It was there before the oldest antiquity but is not old.

— Chuang Tsu

ULTIMATE SOURCES

Return to the source

All things flowed pure and clear out of God. Though often darkly led to evil by passion, I returned, through penance and purification, to the pure fountain—to God—and to your art. In this I was never impelled by selfishness; may it always be so.

— **Ludwig van Beethoven**

The golden house

O come hither, ye Muses, from your golden house. . .

. . . Whose gift of their own work
Hath brought me honor.

— **Sappho**

The storehouse of eternity

The true genius nearly always intrudes and disturbs. He talks to a temporal world out of a world eternal. And thus he says the wrong things at the right time. Eternal truths are never true at any given moment in history. The process of transformation has to reassert itself in order to digest and assimilate the utterly unpractical things that the genius has produced from the storehouse of eternity. Yet the genius is the healer for his time, because anything he betrays of eternal truth is healing.

— **Carl G. Jung**

The secret key

Presumptuous is the artist who does not follow his road through to the end. But chosen are those artists who penetrate to the region of that secret place where primeval power nurtures all evolution.

There, where the power-house of all time and space — call it brain or heart of creation — activates every function; who is the artist who would not dwell there?

In the womb of nature, at the source of creation, where the secret key to all lies guarded.

But not all can enter. Each should follow where the pulse of his own heart leads.

— Paul Klee

Rediscovering that

It is important to realize that that which we are seeking is already there. It is our own right, it is our own nature. It has become obscured by the clouds, and all we are doing is rediscovering *that*. We don't have to go anywhere. We don't have to take a train to anyplace. We just have to come back to our true nature.

—Francis C. Roles

ETERNAL LIGHT

From unity and light

The fundamental beauty of color emerges from unity, coming from shape and the emanation of light which masters the inherent darkness of matter and which is immaterial and yet arises from form and principle.

— Plotinus

The one light above the many

The light possessed by the eyes and the colors possessed by bodies are not enough to make vision complete unless they are aroused and strengthened by the presence and glow of the one light itself above the many, from which the many lights peculiar to the eyes and the bodies were sent out.

— Marsilio Ficino

Light from heaven

Knowledge does not come to us by details, but in flashes of light from heaven.

If by watching all day and all night I may detect some trace of the Ineffable, then will it not be worth the while to watch?

— Henry David Thoreau

As whole and holy

Nothing exists for its own sake, but for a harmony greater than itself, which includes it. A work of art, which accepts this condition, and exists upon its terms, honors the Creation, and so becomes a part of it.

•

The right use of any art or discipline leads *out* of it — as the right use of words leads to a heightened awareness both of the referents of words and of the knowledge, feelings, experiences that cannot be expressed or communicated by words.

•

Because each work of art exists in the world, in reference to or in relation to all other created things, it can have neither no meaning nor a single, literal meaning. Its meanings resonate and accumulate within and among and in response to the meanings of other things.

•

The imagination is our way in to the divine Imagination, permitting us to see wholly — as whole and holy — what we perceive as scattered, as order what we perceive as random.

—Wendell Berry

Part of the making

Nothing is for itself, but each thing partaking of the other is living its greatest possibility, is surpassing itself with vitality and meaning and is part of the making of a great unity.

— Robert Henri

UNITY

An art of the origin

For mastery proves its validity as a form of life, only when it dwells in the boundless Truth and, sustained by it, becomes the art of the origin. The master no longer seeks, but finds. As an artist he is the hieratic man; as a man, the artist, into whose heart, in all his doing and not-doing, working and waiting, being and not-being, the Buddha gazes. The man, the art, the work — it is all one. The art of the inner work, which unlike the outer does not forsake the artist, which he does not "do" and can only "be," springs from depths of which the day knows nothing.

— Eugen Herrigel

A single, original intent

We say a face is beautiful when the precision of its modeling and the disposition of its features reveal proportions we find *harmonious* — harmonious because, deep down, beyond the range of our senses, they produce a resonance, a sort of sounding board that begins to vibrate: a sign of some indefinable absolute operating in the depths of our being.

This sounding board, vibrating in us, is our criterion of harmony. Man must be built upon this axis, in perfect agreement with nature and, probably, the universe — the same organizing axis that seems to underlie all natural phenomena and objects. This axis points to some unifying principle in the universe and a single, original intent.

The laws of physics seem to stem from this axis; we recognize (and love) science and its creations because we sense they are determined by this original intent.

— Le Corbusier

The source of our nourishment

Inspiration is a moment of contact with another reality, the moment when everything at once falls into its proper place, when as it were, the entire structure appears, and every part is seen to be related to the whole. So we cannot deny it exists, nor can we remain indifferent to the experience of this momentary, magical change in our insight. Having had the taste of this other reality (for surely it is not our everyday fare), we yet wait passively for its unpredictable reappearance. We also know that without it we are cut off from the source of our true nourishment, and everything we make is empty, without life, belongs to no organic whole.

— Ilonka Karasz

The ways of heaven

Without going outside, you may know the whole world.
Without looking through the window, you may see the
    ways of heaven.
The farther you go, the less you know.

Thus the sage knows without traveling;
He sees without looking;
He works without doing.

— Lao Tsu

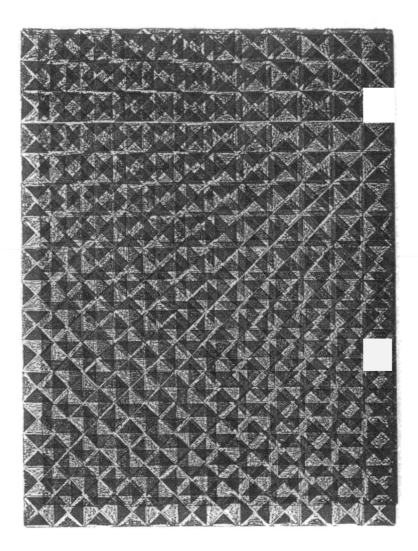

PART II

The Field of
Creative Play

When spirit becomes aware of itself, it wants to play and it creates the beautiful necessity, the field, the atmosphere in which life manifests and recreates. I am nourished by matter. I derive all my strength from the universe: from the sun and the earth and the elements to which my senses are so perfectly attuned.

There is a universal law at work and its justice is instantaneous. I can do as I will only within the confines of these laws of nature. I am compelled to create, to transform matter, but the cause and the reason, the Divine plan, remain hidden. I am an instrument in the progression of human consciousness, and as such my task is clear: to realize truth and beauty, to express the mystery and to hint at the source and to widen the field. I create and wish to leave something in this sacred space to add to the revelation of the Spirit.

COSMOS

Matter, an idea

From the beginning to end all is gripped by the Forms of the Intellectual Realm: Matter itself is held by the Ideas of the elements and to these Ideas are added other Ideas and others again, so that it is hard to work down to crude Matter beneath all that sheathing of Idea. Indeed since Matter itself is, in its degree, an Idea—the lowest — all this universe is Idea and there is nothing that is not Idea as the archetype was. And all is made silently, since nothing had part in the making but Being and Idea —a further reason why creation went without toil. The Exemplar was the Idea of an All and so an All must come into being.

     — Plotinus

Vibrating core of matter

SPACE is the medium by
means of which Form realizes itself.
The potential of extension
                and dimensionality
for structure and Form is inherent
                in the pulsating;
vibrating core of matter.

     — Irene Rice Pereira

Images of the mind

The world is a universal trope of the mind — a symbolic image of it.

     — Novalis

Life-spring of the Cosmos

There is nothing in Mondrian's work that resembles any naturalistic appearance — nothing that even calls to mind by association those things we have considered beautiful. Yet even to one
who has greatly loved the reality and harmony of Nature — the
expanse of sky, the freedom of cloud, the strength of Earth, the
tenderness of life — these beautiful things seem now so empty
in comparison to that beauty of human harmony, which sepa-
rates itself from them, yet contains them all — in all their full
meaning with that much more added — Man's aspiration. How
can it contain them all, having no natural form, no natural
resemblances? Why, because it goes back to the source out of
which evolved the universe, that embryo out of which sprang
finite form — and the full procession of phenomena. And that
dynamic embryo, call it what you will — Order — Harmony —
Truth — Law — is the same life-spring at the back of the Cosmos, as it is at the back of an abstract picture.

— Winifred Nicholson

The great sensible mark

The whole visible world is only an imperceptible atom in the
ample bosom of nature. No idea approaches it. We may enlarge
our conceptions beyond all imaginable space; we only produce
atoms in comparison with the reality of things. It is an infinite
sphere, the center of which is everywhere, the circumference
nowhere. In short it is the greatest sensible mark of the almighty
power of God, that imagination loses itself in that thought.

— Blaise Pascal

13

NATURE

The world is now

All literature is yet to be written. Poetry has scarce chanted its first song. The perpetual admonition of nature to us is, "The world is new, untried. Do not believe the past. I give you the universe a virgin today."

— Ralph Waldo Emerson

Finding the forces

I am attempting to feel the oneness of all, to wipe out the heritage of isolation — it is a lie — man can no more isolate himself than can he isolate a molecule of matter. —Not until I can achieve this knowledge of unity in its entirety — do I feel that I can truly express the forces I feel myself in and part of.

—Burgoyne Diller

Wisdom embodied in nature

A wisdom guides everything that comes into being, whether of nature or craft. This wisdom presides everywhere. Granted that the wisdom of the artist may guide the work and be a sufficient explanation for whatever wisdom shows itself in the arts, but that same wisdom, embodied in the artist, is that wisdom embodied in Nature and is not one constructed of theorems but is a unity, is not a wisdom compiled of diverse parts, but is rather a unity expressing itself in diversity.

— Plotinus

NATURE

Subtle reality

The place . . . or medium of realization is neither mind nor matter, but that intermediate realm of subtle reality which can only be adequately expressed by the symbol. The symbol is neither abstract or concrete, neither rational nor irrational, neither real nor unreal.

— Carl G. Jung

Just behind aspect

This is what it means to be an artist — to seize this essence brooding everywhere in everything, just behind aspect.

— Frank Lloyd Wright

The million disguises

We know the authentic effects of the true fire through every one of its million disguises . . . .

— Ralph Waldo Emerson

Borrowing from matter

Spirit borrows from matter the perceptions on which it feeds and restores them to matter in the form of movements which it has stamped with its own freedom.

—Henri Bergson

NATURE

The external powers

Weight, force and casual impulse, together with resistance, are the four external powers in which all the visible actions of mortals have their being and their end . . . .

Necessity is the mistress and guide of nature. . . . Necessity is the theme and the inventress, the eternal curb and the law of nature . . . .

Experience, the interpreter between formative nature and the human race, teaches how that nature acts among mortals; and being constrained by necessity cannot act otherwise than as reason, which is its helm, requires her to act . . . .

— Leonardo da Vinci

Dark mass of creation

Life's forces and energy
lie hidden in the dark mass
of creation, concealed from man
in the unfathomable recesses
of his being.

— Irene Rice Pereira

NATURE

Nourishing matter

. . . matter is physical exuberance, ennobling contact, virile effort and the joy of growth. It attracts, renews, unites and flowers. By matter we are nourished, lifted up, linked to everything else, invaded by life . . . it contains the spur or the allurement to be our accomplice towards heightened being . . . .

— Teilhard de Chardin

From the finest particles

The power of creativity cannot be named. It remains ultimately mysterious. What does not shake us to our foundations is no mystery. Down to our finest particles we ourselves are changed with this power. We cannot formulate its essence but we can, in some measure, move toward its source . . . . Merged with matter, [this power] must enter into a form that is alive and real. And it is thus that matter takes on life and order, from its smallest particles to its subsidiary rhythms and its higher structures.

— Paul Klee

Hidden nature

Nature loves to hide.
If you do not expect the unexpected, you will not find it; for it is hard to be sought out and difficult.

— Heraclitus

NATURE

Sensing light

I sense light as the giver of all presences, and material as spent Light. What is made by Light casts a shadow, and the shadow belongs to Light. I sense a Threshold: Light to Silence, Silence to Light — an ambiance of inspiration, in which the desire to be, to express, crosses with the possible.

— Louis I. Kahn

Spent light

Material lives by Light . . . . You're spent Light, the mountains are spent Light, the trees are spent Light, the atmosphere is spent Light. All material is spent Light.

— Louis I. Kahn

The hand of nature

Alberto [Giacometti] and I are afflicted with sculpturitis. We work on granite boulders large and small from the moraine of the Forno glacier. Wonderfully polished by time, frost and weather, they are in themselves fantastically beautiful. No human hand can do that. So why not leave the spade work to the elements, and confine ourselves to scratching on them the runes of our own mystery.

— Max Ernst

The great points

The secret to culture is to learn that a few great points steadily reappear . . . and that these few are alone to be regarded; — the escape from all false ties; courage to be what we are, and love of what is simple and beautiful; independence and cheerful relation, these are the essentials, —these, and the wish to serve, to add somewhat to the well-being of men.

— Ralph Waldo Emerson

Humanity's progress

As long as men make life miserable as it often is, Art and Religion are the great supports for spiritual life. But Beauty and Truth then are outside life.

Growing humanity must bring them into life: *Realize Truth and Beauty.* Then life becomes itself Beauty and Truth. Then life itself is Art and Religion. Then Art and Religion are superfluous. But destruction of Art and Religion is not the way: Humanity's *Progress* is the way.

— Piet Mondrian

Evolution of forms

The evolution of consciousness creates form after form — in life as in art. In its evolution of form, art can precede life, in so far as its *form becomes manifestation* — the *natural* becomes *abstract.*

—Piet Mondrian

CULTURE

The principles of growth

All manifestations of art are but landmarks in the progress of the human spirit toward a thing but as yet sensed and far from being possessed . . . .

Art is the inevitable consequence of growth and is the manifestation of the principles of its origin. The work of art is a result; is the output of a progress in development and stands as a record and marks the degree of development . . . . The work is not a finality. It promises more, and from it projection can be made. It is the impress of those who live in full play of their faculties . . . . The impress is made sometimes in material form, as in sculpture or painting, and sometimes in ways more fluid, dispersed, but none the less permanent and none the less revealing of the principles of growth.

— Robert Henri

Between art and life

The question of development of the art spirit in all walks of life interests me. I mean by this, the development of individual judgment and taste, the love of work for the sake of doing things well, tendency toward simplicity and order. If anything can be done to bring the public to a greater consciousness of the relation between art and life, of the part each person plays by exercising and developing his own personal taste and judgment and not depending on outside "authority," it would be well.

— Robert Henri

Civilization imposes

The arts have a development which comes not only from the individual but also from a whole acquired force, the civilization which precedes us. One cannot do just anything. A talented artist cannot do whatever he pleases. If he only used his gifts, he would not exist. We are not the masters of what we produce. It is imposed on us.

— Henri Matisse

Art and play

There is a parallel between art and play. Both must become more *interiorized* as man matures. Play to the child is not simply play: it is his serious occupation and true means of expression. Through play he expresses his feeling for beauty, and realizes his life. As man approaches maturity, play tends to disappear . . . . More and more, the pleasant game becomes "reality." Then, little by little, beauty begins to disappear because material life is incomplete and distorted. Thus, in our time, art is increasingly overwhelmed by the great exigencies of life. But without beauty, life becomes arid.

Like play, art must continue. Both must continue until, in the distant future, mature humanity is able to convey beauty into life and into our material surroundings so that they become more beautiful in themselves. To this end, then, they must be renewed before the past dies and before the future is born.

— Piet Mondrian

CULTURE

Freedom and necessity

Our own existence, like the universe round us, is built up out of Freedom and Necessity in a manner beyond our understanding. Our will is a foreshadowing of what we would do under all circumstances. But circumstances attack us in their own way. The What lies in ourselves, but the How hardly ever depends on us, we dare not ask about the Why and so we are kept, and rightly, to the Because (*quia*).

— Johann Wolfgang von Goethe

The labors of others

A hundred times every day I remind myself that my inner and outer life depend on the labors of other men, living and dead, and that I must exert myself in order to give in the same measure as I have received and am still receiving. . . .

— Albert Einstein

Keeping aloof

Art never harms itself by keeping aloof from the social problems of the day: rather, by doing so, it more completely realizes for us that which we desire.

— Oscar Wilde

Hold to the present

Keep tight hold on the present. Every condition, every moment even, is of infinite worth because it is the representative of all eternity.

— Johann Wolfgang von Goethe

The offering of a day

How to spend a day nobly, is the problem to be solved, beside which all the great reforms which are preached seem to me trivial. If any day has not the privilege of a great action, then at least raise it by a wise passion. If thou canst not do, at least abstain. . . .

— Ralph Waldo Emerson

PART III

The Universal Qualities and Forces of Creativity

*H*ow does anything get created? How does some thing come into being? Ideas form, thoughts arising from the soul within the soul, in consciousness, from the vast reservoir of undifferentiated potential at the heart of matter. Sometimes I am lucky enough to be able to watch an idea forming itself, to see where it wants to go. Modern physics tells us that mere watching brings particles into existence, simply through the act of observation. When I watch well enough, the soul has its way with me.

This attention I give to a forming idea or to the work at hand is a force very much like love. It is a light or a vibration that enlarges me, includes me in a greater circle, enabling me to feel at one with universal forces. This state of being, this health that informs my work, is directly related to beauty, which is not, however, the intent, not the direct aim of the work. Beauty is not something to achieve overtly. If the intent is pure enough, the result will speak of beauty. I will be able to recognize beauty in simplicity, in proportion, in light, in the measure of it within me.

Ignite the soul

Man not only lives on a physical plane,
but also in a world impregnated with
profound and mysterious forces.
These forces flare-up evoking
deep feelings in the heart of man
and ignite his soul with questions
to which his intuition strives to prove
                the answers.
These inquiries flame-up into the
light and bring with them the darkness
                before creation.
Man's senses are aroused by these
                'Unknowns.'
They challenge his imagination
as though holding the key which
unlocks his secret hopes;
                his desires;
                his aspirations;
always leading man on in the quest
                of knowledge.

— **Irene Rice Pereira**

The spirit works as soul

All goes to show that the soul in man is not an organ, but animates and exercises all the organs; is not a function, like the power of memory, of calculation, of comparison, but uses these as hands and feet; is not a faculty, but a light; is not the intellect or the will, but the master of the intellect and the will; is the background of our being, in which they lie, — an immensity not possessed and that cannot be possessed. . . .

When it breathes through his intellect, it is genius: when it breathes through his will, it is virtue; when it flows through his affection, it is love. . . . All reform aims, in some one particular, to let the soul have its way through us; in other words, to engage us to obey. . . .

The soul answers never by words, but by the thing itself that is inquired after. . . .

— Ralph Waldo Emerson

The stream of power

There is a soul at the center of nature, and over the will of every man. . . . There is guidance for each of us, and by lowly listening we shall hear the right word. . . . For you there is a reality, a fit place and congenial duties. Place yourself in the middle of the stream of power and wisdom which animates all whom it floats, and you are without effort impelled to truth, to right, and perfect contentment. . . .

— Ralph Waldo Emerson

Beauty and the soul

If the artist be priest of beauty, nevertheless this beauty is to be sought only according to the principle of the inner need, and can be measured only according to the size and intensity of that need.

That is beautiful which is produced by the inner need, which springs from the soul.

Maeterlink, one of the first warriors, one of the first modern artists of the soul, says: "There is nothing on earth so curious for beauty or so absorbent of it, as soul. For that reason few mortal souls withstand the leadership of a soul which gives to them beauty."

— Wassily Kandinsky

The property of reason

Who looks upon a river in a meditative hour, and is not reminded of the flux of all things? Throw a stone into the stream, and the circles that propagate themselves are the beautiful type of all influence. Man is conscious of a universal soul within or behind his individual life, wherein, as in a firmament, the natures of Justice, Truth, Freedom, arise and shine. This universal soul, he calls Reason: it is not mine or thine or his, but we are its; we are its property and men.

— Ralph Waldo Emerson

SOUL

An impenetrable soul

I remember one vivid winter's day in Versailles. Silence and calm reigned supreme. Everything gazed at me with mysterious, questioning eyes. And then I realized that every corner of the palace, every column, every window possessed a spirit, an impenetrable soul. . . .

— Giorgio De Chirico

The working of the soul

Art, although produced by man's hands, is something not created by hands alone, but something which wells up from a deeper source out of our soul. . . . My sympathies in the literary as well as in the artistic field are drawn most strongly to those artists in whom I see most the working of the soul.

— Vincent van Gogh

Eros

Eros, the love of truth and beauty, is half-god and half-mortal, in contact with both evil and the good at the same time. And the aim of this striving, called *eros*, is to merge with reality itself, beauty and goodness themselves, in order to conceive and give birth to virtue and wisdom in the soul.

— Jacob Needleman

LOVE

Nothing but love

Love is justly called Ruler of the Arts, for a man fashions works of art carefully and completes them thoroughly, who esteems highly both the works themselves and the people for whom they are made. There is, then, this fact, that artists in each of the arts seek after and care for nothing but love.

— Marsilio Ficino

The genius of love

Love is himself so divine a poet that he can kindle in the souls of others the poetic fire, for no matter what dull clay we seemed to be before, we are every one of us a poet when we are in love. We need ask no further proof than this that Love is a poet deeply versed in every branch of what I may define succinctly as creative art, for, just as no one can give away what he has not got, so no one can teach what he does not know.

And who will deny that the creative power by which all living things are begotten and brought forth is the very genius of Love? Do we not, moreover, recognize that in every art and craft the artist and the craftsman who work under the direction of this same god achieve the brightest fame, while those that lack his influence grow old in the shadow of oblivion?

— Plato

My love depends

O truant Muse, what shall be thy amends
For thy neglect of truth in beauty dy'd?
Both truth and beauty on my love depends;
So dost thou too, and therein dignified.
Make answer, Muse. Wilt thou not haply say
'Truth needs no color with his color fix'd;
Beauty no pencil, beauty's truth to lay;
But best is best, if never intermix'd'?
Because he need no praise, wilt thou be dumb?
Excuse not silence so; for't lies in thee
To make him much outlive a gilded tomb,
and to be prais'd of ages yet to be.
Then do thy office, Muse. I teach thee how
To make him seem, long hence, as he shows now.

— **William Shakespeare**

LOVE

The heart naturally loves

The heart has its reason, which reason does not know. We feel it in a thousand things. I say that the heart naturally loves the Universal Being, and also itself naturally, according as it gives itself to them; and it hardens itself against one or the other at its will. You have rejected the one, and kept the other. Is it by reason that you love yourself?

— Blaise Pascal

Love and Truth together

So it is much better to cut through the thought processes and analysis, and go for peace and this state where a feeling of love arises together with a sudden sharp feeling of truth. The two arise together very often, and this emotional realization of truth, which could be called intuition, is a very great thing.

—Francis C. Roles

The principles

Three things are needed for beauty: wholeness, harmony, and radiance.

— Thomas Aquinas

The deeper love

Beauty must always induce the spirit of wonder and a delectable affliction, a delight causing a trembling of love and longing. This feeling applies to the invisible as much as to the visible in every soul, in some degree, but most especially to those who are more disposed to this deeper love — as is the case with those stabbed with delight at the beauty of the body, those being called lovers who feel the deepest wounds.

— Plotinus

The most ascending quality

I am warned by the ill fate of many philosophers not to attempt a definition of Beauty. I will rather enumerate a few of its qualities. We ascribe beauty to that which is simple; which has no superfluous parts; which exactly answers its end; which stands related to all things; which is the mean of many extremes. It is the most enduring quality, and the most ascending quality.

— Ralph Waldo Emerson

BEAUTY

Clarity and grace

The beauty of bodies does not consist in the shadow of materiality, but in the clarity and gracefulness of form, not in the hidden bulk, but in a kind of luminous harmony, not in an inert and stupid weight, but in a fitting number and measure. Light, gracefulness, proportion, number, and measure which we apprehend by thought, vision, and hearing [are the beautiful]. It is toward these that the true ardor of the genuine lover strives.

— Marsilio Ficino

A necessary satisfaction

Taste is the faculty of judging of an object or a method of representing it by an *entirely disinterested* satisfaction or dissatisfaction. The object of such satisfaction is called *beautiful*.

The *beautiful* is that which pleases universally without [requiring] a concept.

Beauty is the form of the *purposiveness* of an object, so far as this is perceived in it *without any representation of a purpose*.

The *beautiful* is that which without any concept is cognized as the object of a *necessary* satisfaction.

— Immanuel Kant

That life above all others

He who has been instructed thus far in the things of love, and who has learned to see the beautiful in due order and succession, when he comes toward the end will suddenly perceive a nature of wondrous beauty (and this, Socrates, is the final cause of all our former toils) — a nature which in the first place is everlasting, not growing and decaying, or waxing and waning; secondly, not fair in one point of view and foul in another, or at one time or in one relation or at one place fair, at another time or in another relation or at another place foul . . . but beauty absolute, separate, simple, and everlasting, which without diminution and without increase, or any change, is imparted to the ever-growing and perishing beauties of all other things. . . .This, my dear Socrates. . . . is that life above all others which man should live, in the contemplation of beauty absolute; a beauty which if you once beheld, you would see not to be after the measure of gold, and garments, and fair boys and youths. . . . But what if man had eyes to see the true beauty — the divine beauty. . . . and holding converse with the true beauty simple and divine. . . . Would that be an ignoble life?

— Plato

The mystery of life

When I think of art I think of beauty. Beauty is the mystery of life. It is not in the eye, it is in the mind. In our minds there is awareness of perfection

— Agnes Martin

BEAUTY

Longing in the heart

Beauty in the heart that longs for it is more sublime than in the eyes of him who sees it. . . .

— Kahlil Gibran

Flowing from the Divine

But where the Ideal-Form has entered, it has grouped and coordinated what from a diversity of parts was to become a unit: it has rallied confusion into cooperation: it has made the sum one harmonious coherence: for the Idea is a unity and what it molds must come to unify as far as multiplicity may.

And on what has thus been compacted to unity, Beauty enthrones itself, giving itself to the parts as to the sum: when it lights on some natural unity, a thing of like parts, then it gives itself to that whole. Thus, for an illustration, there is the beauty, conferred by craftsmanship, of all a house with all its parts, and the beauty which some natural quality may give to a single stone.

This, then, is how the material thing becomes beautiful — by communicating in the thought that flows from the divine.

— Plotinus

The beautiful shines

In German the word beautiful (*das Schoene*) is related to shining (*das Scheinende*). The beautiful shines; brings its inner nature to the surface. It is the distinguishing quality of the beautiful not to hide itself, but to carry its essence into outer configuration. Thus beauty reveals inwardness through outer form; a shining radiates outward into the World.

— Rudolf Steiner

Higher than nature

We may. . . . begin at once by asserting that artistic beauty stands *higher* than nature. For the beauty of art is a beauty that is born — born again, that is — of the mind; and by as much as the mind and its products are higher than nature and its appearances, by so much is the beauty of art higher than the beauty of nature.

— G. W. F. Hegel

Illumining human sight

. . .
Spiritual beauty illuminating human sight
Lines with its passion and mystery Matter's mask
And squanders eternity on a beat of Time.
. . .

— Sri Aurobindo

BEAUTY

Our human heritage

This inborn love of beauty, our human heritage, *must* find expression if we are to be happy. If the hunger for beauty remains unsatisfied, the effects are seen in loss of physical and mental health, so deep is the need. . . .

— H. E. Huntley

. . . a joy forever

Beauty is the only thing that time cannot harm. Philosophies fall away like sand, and creeds follow one another like the withered leaves of Autumn; but what is beautiful is a joy for all seasons and a possession for all eternity.

— Oscar Wilde

An indeterminate end

Beauty in the master craftsman's atelier is not a final cause of the work to be done, but an inevitable accident. And for this reason, that the work of art is always occasional; it is the nature of a rational being to work for particular ends, whereas beauty is an indeterminate end; whether the artist is planning a picture, a song or a city, he has in view to make that thing and nothing else.

— Ananda K. Coomaraswamy

The poet's labor

For the essence and the end
Of his labor is beauty, for goodness and evil are two things and
yet variant, but the quality of life as of death and of light.
As of darkness is one, one beauty, the rhythm of the Wheel, and
who can behold it is happy and will praise it to the people.

— Robinson Jeffers

The final standard

When I am working on a problem, I never think about beauty.
I think only how to solve the problem. But when I have finished, if the solution is not beautiful, I know it is wrong.

— Buckminster Fuller

Inner judgment

Within each soul is a faculty belonging to beauty, certain of its
perception when the entire soul is called upon to affirm its
judgments.

— Plotinus

40

PART IV

The Flowering of Creative Energy

*M*oved by the forces of nature, by an inner necessity, by desire or a feeling, I want to play. I want to create. Creative energy is very pure and very raw — essence wanting to become matter but still formless. I must not name or grasp it; it is very subtle and new, and I must not filter it through the mental construct of ego.

Instead, I wait, and waiting holds in check the scanning of the mind, the fears, the doubts, the devils which are the past. I sit and I wait, and again and again the attention wanders off — the mind is fabricating, visualizing, searching for the "tried and true."

At an instant the creative energy explodes — my essence, knowledge, and inspiration confer and present the mind with a clear new idea — a cord is struck in the heart and reverberates through the instrument. I must hold fast to this vision which wants to find expression.

Conception

Genesis eternal

I would like now to examine the dimensions of the object in a new light and so try to show how it is that the artist frequently arrives at what appears to be such an arbitrary "deformation" of natural forms.

First, he does not attach such intense importance to natural form as do so many realist critics, because, for him, these final forms are not the real stuff of the process of natural creation. For he places more value on the powers which do the forming than on the final forms themselves. . . .

Thus he surveys with penetrating eye the finished forms which nature places before him.

The deeper he looks, the more readily he can extend his view from the present to the past, the more deeply he is impressed by the one essential image of creation itself, as Genesis, rather than by the image of nature, the finished product.

Then he permits himself the thought that the process of creation can today hardly be complete and he sees the act of world creation stretching from the past to the future. Genesis eternal!

— Paul Klee

Born of spirit

. . . [Diotima speaking] But those whose procreancy is of the spirit rather than of the flesh — and they are not unknown, Socrates — conceive and bear the things of the spirit. And what are they? you ask. Wisdom and all her sister virtues; it is the office of every poet to beget them, and of every artist whom we may call creative.

— Plato

A song comes

And my journal is such a womb. I sit in it with my limbs and belly and my thoughts and my dreams. But I sit in the dark for a long time and don't recognize that I have already given birth to myself — until a song comes out of me, a dream, a vision, a sudden flash of recognition of my wholeness. And I realize that all along I have been giving birth to my creations, my text, children, even while I did not recognize my own shape yet.

— Burghild Nina Holzer

Beginning to awaken

If I could really paint! A month ago I was so sure of what I wanted. Inside me I saw it out there, walked around with it like a queen, and was blissful. Now the veils have fallen again, gray veils, hiding the whole idea from me. I stand like a beggar at the door, shivering in the cold, pleading to be let in. It is hard to move patiently, step by step, when one is young and demanding. Now I'm beginning to awaken as a human being. I'm becoming a woman. The child in me is beginning to recognize life, the purpose of a woman; and it awaits fulfillment. It will be beautiful, full of wonder.

— Paula Modersohn-Becker

CONCEPTION

An urgent revelation

We must hold enormous faith in ourselves: it is essential that the revelation we receive, the conception of an image which embraces a certain thing, which has no sense of itself, which has no subject, which means *absolutely nothing* from the logical point of view — I repeat, it is essential that such a revelation or conception should speak so strongly in us, evoke such agony or joy, that we feel compelled to paint, compelled by an impulse even more urgent than the hungry desperation which drives a man to tearing at a piece of bread like a savage beast.

— Giorgio De Chirico

Filling the gaps

Creation is the reason for existence, the state of divinity in humanity. Creation is the streamlining of transcendence into the deficiencies of our rough, turbulent world. The initial step of the creative role is fulfilled by understanding the nature of these deficiencies. The second is filling these gaps with wisdom, so that the real world will conform to the ideal world.

— Gilah Yelin Hirsch

Art and nature collaborate

Art arises when the secret vision of the artist and the manifestation of nature agree to find new shapes. . . .

— Kahlil Gibran

The creative moment

Man is by nature a *creator*. After the likeness of his Maker, man is born to create: to fashion beauty, to originate new values. This truth awakens a resonant response deep within us, for we know that one of the most intense joys that the soul of man can experience is that of creative activity. Ask the artist. Ask the poet. Ask the scientist. Ask the inventor or my neighbor who grows prize roses. They all know the deep spiritual satisfaction associated with the moment of orgasm of creation . . . .

— H. E. Huntley

Birth of new ideas

I work better when I am not working than when I am, like Saint-Pol Roux who used to put a notice outside his door, LE POETE TRAVAILLE, when he intended to sleep.

The atmosphere which favors this tension [that gives birth to new ideas], I find in poetry, music, architecture... in my daily walk, in certain noises: the noise of the horses in the country, the creaking of wooden cartwheels, footsteps, cries in the night, crickets. The spectacle of the sky overwhelms me. . . . Empty spaces, empty horizons, empty plains — everything that is bare has always greatly impressed me.

— Joan Miró

CONCEPTION

The invitation

I loaf and invite my soul,
I learn and loaf at my ease . . . observing a spear of summer grass.

— Walt Whitman

A whole new geography

And one day I tried to arrive at silence directly, more resignedly, offering myself up to the fate that governs all profound struggle. Those millions of furious clawings were transformed into millions of grains of dust, of sand. . . . A whole new landscape, as in the story of one who goes through the looking glass, opened before me as if to communicate the most secret innerness of things. A whole new geography illumined me from surprise to surprise. A suggestion of rare combinations and molecular structures, of atomic phenomena from the world of galaxies, or from microscopic images.

— Antoni Tàpies

From unity

Inspiration is in seeing a part of the whole with the part of the whole in you.

— Kahlil Gibran

CONCEPTION

Dawn in her womb

The Stars are Playing in the Skies
The Earth's Asleep —
One Soul's Awake
A woman
               The Stars Beckon —
Her Room is a Whiteness
Whiteness Opens its Door
She walks into Darkness
Alone
With the Night — alone with the Stars
A Mountain nearby
Its peak near those stars —
She climbs the Steep Mountain
Alone —
To the Top
        The Woman Walks Homeward
        To her Little White Room
        No longer Alone
        She Carries Dawn
        In Her Womb

      — Alfred Stieglitz

FORCES

The rational impulse

The universal demand for artistic expression is based on the rational impulse in man's nature to exalt both the world of his soul experience and that of Nature for himself into the conscious embrace of mind as an object in which he rediscovers himself. He satisfies the demand of this spiritual freedom by making explicit to his *inner* life all that exists, no less than from the further point of view giving a realized *external* embodiment to the self made thus explicit. And by this reduplication of what is his own he places before the vision and within the cognition of himself and others what is within him. This is the free rationality of man, in which art as also all action and knowledge originates.

— G. W. F. Hegel

Genius, a force of nature

Genius is the talent which gives the rule to art. Since talent, as the innate productive faculty of the artist, belongs itself to nature, we may express the matter thus: Genius is the innate mental disposition through which nature gives the rule to art.

— Immanuel Kant

Grace and free will

When they are properly understood the law of grace and the law of free will are not at all contradictory; both belong to a single whole and often need each other.

— Novalis

The inner urge

At a certain time what is inevitable ripens, that is, the creative *spirit* (which could be called the abstract spirit) makes contact with the soul, later with other souls, and awakens a yearning, an inner urge.

When the conditions necessary for the maturation of a certain form are met, the yearning, the inner urge, the force is strengthened so that it can create a new value in the human spirit that consciously or unconsciously begins to live in man.

Consciously or unconsciously man tries, from this moment on, to find a material form for the spiritual form, for the new value that lives within him.

This is the search by the spiritual value for materialization. Matter is a kind of larder from which the spirit chooses what is *necessary* for itself, much as a cook would.

This is the positive, the creative. This is goodness. *The white, fertilizing ray.*

This white ray leads to evolution, to elevation. Behind matter, within matter, the creative spirit is hidden.

— Wassily Kandinsky

FORCES

New ray of peace

In vain I look for change abroad
　　And can no difference find,
Till some new ray of peace uncalled
　　Illumes my inmost mind.

— Henry Thoreau

Innate talent

The essential plasticity and material element in a work of art is
subjectively present in the artist as part of his native disposition
and impulse, and as his unconscious activity belongs in part to
that which man receives straight from Nature. No doubt the
entire talent and genius of an individual is not wholly exhausted by what we describe as natural capability. The creation of art
is quite as much a spiritual and self-cognized process; but for
all that we affirm that its spirituality contains an element of
plastic or configurative facility which Nature confers on it. For
this reason, though almost anybody can reach a certain point
in art, yet, in order to pass beyond this — and it is here that the
art in question really begins — a talent for art which is inborn
and of a higher order altogether is indispensable.

— G. W. F. Hegel

FORCES

Conscious attention

Attention is an independent force which will not be manipulated by one's part. Cleared of all internal noise, conscious attention is an instrument which vibrates like a crystal at its own frequency. It is free to receive the signals broadcast at each moment from a creative universe in communication with all creatures. . . .

Attention is the quintessential medium to reveal man's dormant energies to himself. . . .

— William Segal

Undivided attention

To everything that man undertakes he must give his undivided attention, his self; once he has done this, miraculously thoughts arise, or a new kind of perceptions, which appear to be nothing more than delicate, abrupt movements of colored pencil, or strange contractions and figurations of an elastic fluid. . . .

— Novalis

Coming alive

When the artist is alive in any person, whatever his kind of work may be, he becomes an inventive, searching, daring, self-expressing creature. He becomes interesting to other people. He disturbs, upsets, enlightens, and he opens ways for a better understanding.

— Robert Henri

51

The enchantment of the heart

The instant wherein that supreme quality of beauty, the clear radiance of the esthetic image, is apprehended luminously by the mind which has been arrested by its wholeness and fascinated by its harmony is the luminous silent stasis of esthetic pleasure, a spiritual state very like to that cardiac condition which the Italian physiologist Luigi Galvani, using a phrase almost as beautiful as Shelley's, called the enchantment of the heart.

— James Joyce

Grace and inspiration

The notion of grace, as opposed to virtue depending on the will, and that of inspiration, as opposed to intellectual or artistic work, these two notions, if they are well understood, show the efficacy of desire and of waiting.

— Simone Weil

Enthusiasm

Enthusiasm is a volcano on whose top never grows the grass of hesitation. . . .

— Kahlil Gibran

STATES

A fine frenzy rolling

The poet's eye, in a fine frenzy rolling,
Doth glance from heaven to earth, from earth to heaven;
And as imagination bodies forth
The forms of things unknown, the poet's pen
Turns them to shapes and gives to airy nothing
A local habitation and a name.

— William Shakespeare

Ecstasy

Our ecstatic states, which appear to yield so little fruit, have this value at least: though in the seasons when our genius reigns we may be powerless for expression, yet, in calmer seasons, when our talent is active, the memory of those rarer moods comes to color our picture and is the permanent paintpot, as it were, into which we dip our brush. Thus no life or experience goes unreported at last; but if it be not solid gold it is gold-leaf, which gilds the furniture of the mind. It is an experience of infinite beauty on which we unfailingly draw, which enables us to exaggerate ever truly. Our moments of inspiration are not lost though we have no particular poem to show for them; for those experiences have left an indelible impression, and we are ever and anon reminded of them.

— Henry David Thoreau

STATES

Abandonment

The one thing which we seek with insatiable desire, is to forget ourselves, to be surprised out of our propriety, to lose our sempiternal memory, and to do something without knowing how or why; in short to draw a new circle. Nothing great was ever achieved without enthusiasm. The way of life is wonderful: it is abandonment. . . . "A man," said Oliver Cromwell, "never rises so high as when he knows not whither he is going." . . .

— Ralph Waldo Emerson

An irresistible longing

The beautiful is a manifestation of the secret laws of nature. . . . When nature begins to reveal her open secret to a person, he feels an irresistible longing for her most worthy interpreter, art.

— Johann Wolfgang von Goethe

Feeling, an inward light

Will he ever learn to feel? This divine, most natural of all senses is but little known to him. Yet feeling would bring back the old time for which we yearn. The element of feeling is an inward light that breaks into stronger, more beautiful colors. If one could feel truly, then stars would rise within one; one would learn to feel the whole world. . . .

— Novalis

The secret of sensation

To create forms means: to live. Are not children more creative in drawing directly from the secret of their sensations than the imitator of Greek forms? . . .

— August Macke

Receptivity

The receptivity of the artist must never be confused with passivity. Receptivity is the artist's holding him — or herself alive and open to hear what being may speak. Such receptivity requires a nimbleness, a fine-honed sensitivity in order to let one's self be the vehicle of whatever vision may emerge. It is the opposite of the authoritarian demands impelled by "will power." An artist's "waiting". . . requires a high degree of attention, as when a diver is poised on the end of the springboard, not jumping but holding his or her muscles in sensitive balance for the right second. It is an active listening, keyed to hear the answer, alert to see whatever can be glimpsed when the vision or the words do come. It is a waiting for the birthing process to begin to move in its own organic time. It is necessary that the artist have this sense of timing, that he or she respect these periods of receptivity as part of the mystery of creativity and creation.

— Rollo May

STATES

Waiting, not seeking

Active searching is prejudicial, not only to love, but also to the intelligence, whose laws are the same as those of love. We just have to wait for the solution of a geometrical problem or the meaning of a Latin or Greek sentence to come into our mind. Still more must we wait for any new scientific truth or for a beautiful line of poetry. Seeking leads us astray. This is the case of every form of what is truly good. . . . This waiting for goodness and truth is, however, something more intense than any searching.

— Simone Weil

Heightened perception

The more the student ascends in his conception of the world, the more does his development in the observation and perception of nature help him to the free creation of abstract forms, which, by the way of the willed-schematic, reach a new naturalness, the naturalness of the work. He then creates a work, or takes part in the creation of works that are a simile to the work of God.

— Paul Klee

To feel the pull

Happiness is being on the beam with life — to feel the pull of life.

— Agnes Martin

STATES

This is the state. . . .

When some external cause or inward disposition lifts us suddenly out of the endless stream of willing, delivers knowledge from
the slavery of the will, the attention is no longer directed to the
motives of willing, but comprehends things free from their relation to the will, and thus observes them without personal interest, without subjectivity, purely objectively, gives itself entirely up
to them so far as they are ideas, but not in so far as they are
motives. . . .

. . . this is the state . . . necessary for the knowledge of
the Idea, as pure contemplation, as sinking oneself in perception, losing oneself in the object, forgetting all individuality,
surrendering the kind of knowledge which follows the principle
of sufficient reason, and comprehends only relations; the state
by means of which at once and inseperably the perceived particular thing is raised to the Idea of its whole species, and the
knowing individual to the pure subject of will-less knowledge,
and as such they are both taken out of the stream of time and
all other relations. It is then all one whether we see the sun set
from the prison or from the palace.

— Arthur Schopenhauer

ACTION

Spiritual energy apparent

The ray of light passes invisible through space, and only when it falls on an object, is it seen. So your spiritual energy is barren and useless until it is directed on something outward: then it is a thought: the relation between you and it first makes you, the Value of you, apparent to me. . . .

—Ralph Waldo Emerson

Gifts of the moment

Quite simple things can lead to discovery. This is what I would like to do with painting: starting with simple things, to lead the eye by various manipulations of colors, objects and tensions toward a transformation and a reward.

My wish is to make something permanent out of the transitory, by means at once dramatic and colloquial. Certain moments have the gift of revealing the past and foretelling the future. It is these moments that I hope to catch.

— Loren MacIver

The mind plays

The creation of something new is not accomplished by the intellect but by the play instinct acting from inner necessity. The creative mind plays with the objects it loves.

— C. G. Jung

ACTION

Quickened to the instant

And then there is inspiration. Where does it come from? Mostly from the excitement of living. I get it from the diversity of a tree or the ripple of the sea, a bit of poetry, the sighting of a dolphin breaking the still water and moving toward me . . . anything that quickens you to the instant. And whether one would call this inspiration or necessity, I really do not know.

— Martha Graham

The beloved object

The lover is moved by the beloved object as the senses are by the sensible objects; and they unite and become one and the same thing. The work is the first thing born of this union; if the thing loved is base the lover becomes base.

When the thing taken into union is perfectly adapted to that which receives it, the result is delight and pleasure and satisfaction.

When that which loves is united to the thing beloved it can rest there; when the burden is laid down it finds rest there. . . .

— Leonardo da Vinci

ACTION

Pinnacles of experience

There are moments in our lives, there are moments in a day, when we seem to see beyond the usual. Such are the moments of our greatest wisdom.

At such times there is a song going on within us, a song to which we listen. It fills us with surprise. We marvel at it. . . . It is aristocratic and will not associate itself with the commonplace. . . . We live in the memory of these songs which in moments of intellectual inadvertance have been possible to us. They are the pinnacles of our experience and it is the desire to express these intimate sensations, this song from within, which motivates the masters of all art.

— Robert Henri

Leap after leap

Living is a form of not being sure, not knowing what next or how. The moment you know how, you begin to die a little. The artist never entirely knows. We guess. We may be wrong, but we take leap after leap in the dark.

— Agnes De Mille

ACTION

Tended with absurd care

My center does not come from my mind — it feels in me like a plot of warm moist well-tilled earth with the sun shining hot on it — . . . It seems I would rather feel starkly empty than let anything be planted that cannot be tended to the fullest possibility of its growth. . . . I do know that the demands of my plot of earth are relentless if anything is to grow in it — worthy of its quality. . . . If the past year or two or three has taught me anything it is that my plot of earth must be tended with absurd care. . . .

— Georgia O'Keeffe

There is only one of you

There is a vitality, a life force, an energy, a quickening, that is translated through you into action, and because there is only one of you in all time, this expression is unique. And if you block it, it will never exist through any other medium and will be lost.

— Martha Graham

PART V

The Faculties of Creative Expression

The senses play among the sense objects and inform the mind of time and place; they behold the beauty of Creation and nourish mind and heart. The senses are the bridge between the inner and the outer world, and I treasure this gift and delight in the sensations and emotions it evokes. I am the observer; mind is everywhere, within and without. I see mind in the perfect geometry of a flower, in the structure of a bone; I see mind in the masterworks of art and hear mind in music.

"There is one mind common to all individual men," says Emerson, and I participate in this vast realm. When a thought arises from a source unknown, the intellect holds it fast and examines it; discrimination judges and weighs. My imagination can run with it, as visualization presents it to my inner eye. My heart, my intuition, my inner resources, all conspire and illumine the mind and what it beholds. Beauty is in the mind as is number and geometry and light. I am an instrument endowed with awareness, I am the hands and eyes of the Great Mind. Through mind and its faculties, I create new worlds. I transform gross energy into fine essence; I question and search and examine my life.

Consciousness: the final reference

Consciousness is either with us and we are alive, or it is not, and then we are not in a state of living; to be alive means to be awake and to have the full power which consciousness gives us to create, control, and co-ordinate.

. . . We know of no other source of experiences, be they events outside ourselves or within us, except our consciousness of them. Neither do we have any other frame of reference for evaluating, controlling, or co-ordinating what we do.

Feeling alone or senses and reason by themselves cannot provide such a frame of reference; feeling may lead us astray, senses may deceive, reason may err — but our consciousness as the sum total of all these faculties together is our final frame of reference for all our experiences and all our creations.

Co-ordination is the essential drive of our consciousness, and co-ordination is the form of its structure, the guiding pattern of its operation in us; and as the source of all the creations of man, consciousness does not tolerate amorphous deformities; having the unique faculty of being conscious of itself, it is able to create images of new experiences the origin of which escapes our direct observation.

— Naum Gabo

Meditative awareness

When we have meditative awareness we know how to touch each experience, and consequently we do not get pulled in and trapped by expectations, disappointments, or disillusionments.

— Tarthang Tulku

All is consciousness

There is only one Consciousness. The levels are levels of impediment to that Consciousness. *Everything* is that Consciousness. That is what we have to feel and know.

— Francis C. Roles

It moves by law

. . . everywhere consciousness prevails. In fact everything is conscious. . . . Nothing moves without consciousness and consciousness does not move by chance; it moves by law—the law of cause and effect. If one adheres to the law of chance one is depriving oneself of the law of consciousness.

— H.H. Shantanand Saraswati

CONSCIOUSNESS

Timeless being

See beyond the beginning — not to an earlier time — but to timeless being. See beyond the end, not to going on to another plane or place — but see to that consciousness of existence that supersedes time and includes all the good of what we think of as Past, Present, Future — but not necessarily in that order.

Work out one's human life concept in the light of timeless being. Take time out of the concept of things we call matter, and matter would disintegrate or disappear. Any attempt to erase matter out of our concept of being without eliminating time, and we are still buried in material conceptions.

— **Winifred Nicholson**

The conscious mind at work

But though the non-logical, instinctive, subconscious part of the mind must play its part in his work, he also has a conscious mind which is not inactive. The artist works with a concentration of his whole personality, and the conscious part of it resolves conflicts, organizes memories, and prevents him from trying to walk in two directions at the same time.

— **Henry Moore**

Indivisible consciousness

I believe that human consciousness is a growing force given to us with life, and that its growth is as yet far, far indeed, from reaching its potential limits. It is a force which cannot be broken up into pieces and parts. It does not depend on any one individual's wanton will and whim. It grows and perfects itself with a power all its own.

It is within us, and our life is sustained by it. Human life without its presence is not only meaningless, it is not human. Its presence is revealed to us not by our experiences alone but by the images and conceptions which our consciousness enables us to create as a guide for our action.

— Naum Gabo

Faith in intuition

To believe your own thought, to believe that what is true for you in your private heart, is true for all men, — that is genius. Speak your latent conviction and it shall be the universal sense; for the inmost in due time becomes the outmost . . . . A man should learn to detect and watch that gleam of light which flashes across his mind from within, more than the luster of the firmament of bards and sages . . . . In every work of genius we recognize our own rejected thoughts: they come back to us with a certain alienated majesty . . . .

Every man discriminates between the voluntary acts of his mind, and his involuntary perceptions, and knows that to his involuntary perceptions a perfect faith is due . . . .

— Ralph Waldo Emerson

ASPECTS OF MIND

Understanding, reason, and the world

Space, time, society, labor, climate, food, locomotion, the animals, the mechanical forces, give us sincerest lessons, day by day, whose meaning is unlimited. They educate both the understanding and the Reason. Every property of matter is a school for the understanding, — its solidity or resistance, its inertia, its extension, its figure, its divisibility. The understanding adds, divides, combines, measures, and finds everlasting nutriment and room for its activity in this worthy scene. Meantime, Reason transfers all these lessons into its own world of thought, by perceiving the analogy that marries Matter and Mind.

— Ralph Waldo Emerson

Clarity of mind

The mind is a tool, it is either clogged, bound, rusty, or it is a clear way to and from the soul. An artist should not be afraid to know . . . .

— Robert Henri

Listening to the mind

When you look in your mind you find it covered with a lot of rubbishy thoughts. You have to penetrate these and hear what your mind is telling you to do. Such work is original work. All other work made from ideas is not inspired and it is not art work.

— Agnes Martin

The gift of understanding

The truth is that sincerity in art is not an affair of will, of a moral choice between honesty and dishonesty. It is mainly an affair of talent . . . . For in matters of art "being sincere," is synonymous with "possessing the gifts of psychological understanding and expression."

All human beings feel very much the same emotions; but few know exactly what they feel or can divine the feelings of others. Psychological insight is a special faculty, like the faculty for understanding mathematics or music. And of the few who possess that faculty only two or three in every hundred are born with the talent of expressing their knowledge in artistic form.

— Aldous Huxley

Ideas, not concepts

The formation of conceptualized ideas occurs when the ordinary intellect takes over the formulations of real ideas and converts them into concepts. When this happens, the part of the mind that longs for inner truth has already been left behind . . . . "Unity" of ordinary thought and ordinary emotion is precisely the enemy of truth. This authentic structural unity of human nature is, however, possible only with the development in man of an attention that can make contact with all the parts of the self. This attention first appears only when I myself am in question in the midst of life. The first function of real ideas is not to unite the parts of us into a superficial harmony, but to separate them — that is, to break down the deceptive unity called ego.

— Jacob Needleman

ASPECTS OF MIND

The light of the imagination

If I had not carried the world in my imagination beforehand, my seeing eyes would have been blind and all my effort and experience nothing but dead and useless trouble. The light is there and the colors are all round us, but if we had no light and no color in our own eyes we could never be aware of them outside us.

— Johann Wolfgang von Goethe

Art made noble by the mind

True art is made noble and religious by the mind producing it. . . . The mind, the soul, becomes ennobled by the endeavor to create something perfect, for God is perfection, and whoever strives after perfection is striving for something divine.

— Michelangelo

Know the intellect

Plato, I believe, said that beauty is the splendor of truth. I don't think that it has a meaning but the true and the beautiful are akin. Truth is beheld by the intellect which is appeased by the most satisfying relations of the intelligible: beauty is beheld by the imagination which is appeased by the most satisfying relations of the sensible. The first step in the direction of truth is to understand the frame and scope of the intellect itself, to comprehend the act itself of intellection.

— James Joyce

Letting the mind do its work

When given an assignment, I have a habit of committing it *to memory* by not allowing myself to make any sketches for several months. The human mind is, by nature, fairly autonomous. It is a container into which we can pour the elements of a problem helter-skelter and let them float, simmer, and ferment for a while. Then, one day, a spontaneous inner impulse triggers a reaction. We pick up a pencil, a piece of charcoal, or a colored pencil (color is the key to this process) and put it down on paper. The idea, or child, emerges. It has come into the world; *it has been born.*

—Le Corbusier

The union of imagination and understanding

Thus genius properly consists in the happy relation [between imagination and understanding],which no science can teach and no industry can learn, by which ideas are found for a given concept; and, on the other hand, we thus find for these ideas the expression by means of which the subjective state of mind brought about by them, as an accompaniment of the concept, can be communicated to others. The latter talent is, properly speaking, what is called spirit; for to express the ineffable element in the state of mind implied by a certain representation and to make it universally communicable — whether the expression be in speech or painting or statuary — this requires a faculty of seizing the quickly passing play of imagination and of unifying it in a concept that can be communicated without any constraint.

— Immanuel Kant

All the attributes

The best of beauty is a finer charm than skill in surfaces, in out-
lines, or rules of art can ever teach, namely, a radiation from the
work of art of human character, — a wonderful expression
through stone or canvas or musical sound of the deepest and
simplest attributes of our nature, and therefore most intelligible
at last to those souls which have these attributes. . . .

— Ralph Waldo Emerson

Taste, a faculty of mind

To carry out a work of art it is not enough to know the relations
of color and form and to apply the laws that govern them; the
artist must also contrive to free himself from the servitude inherent in such a task. Any painter of healthy sensitivity and sufficient intelligence can provide us with well-painted pictures; but
only he can awaken beauty who is designated by Taste. We call
thus the faculty thanks to which we become conscious of Quality, and we reject the notions of good taste and bad taste which
correspond with nothing positive: a faculty is neither good nor
bad; it is simply more or less developed.

— Albert Gleizes and Jean Metzinger

The human lyre

Studying the secrets of music, we can discover what the Greeks, who knew a great deal about these matters, meant by the lyre of Apollo. What is experienced musically is really man's hidden adaptation to the inner harmonic-melodic relationships of cosmic existence out of which he was shaped. His nerve fibers, ramifications of the spinal cord, are marvelous musical strings with a metamorphosed activity. The spinal cord culminating in the brain, and distributing its nerve fibers throughout the body, is the lyre of Apollo. Upon these nerve fibers the soul-spirit man is "played" within the earthly sphere. Thus man himself is the world's most perfect instrument; and he can experience artistically the tones of an external musical instrument to the degree that he feels this connection between the sounding of strings of a new instrument, for example, and his own coursing blood and nerve fibers. In other words, man, as nerve man, is inwardly built up of music, and feels it artistically to the degree that he feels its harmonization with the mystery of his own musical structure.

— Rudolf Steiner

Discrimination, the most precious virtue

. . . Reflective virtue is simply an acquired clarity of the intellect, and moral virtue is constant warmth of heart kindled by that clarity. We should remember that of the human virtues none is more precious than discrimination . . . . For everything is an obstacle and nothing of use to a man who cannot distinguish the good from the bad and separate the bad from the good. . . .
— Marsilio Ficino

EMOTION

Reason and feeling in one

For *consciousness* in art is another new contemporary character-istic: the artist is no longer a blind tool of intuition. *Natural feel-ing* no longer dominates the work of art, which expresses *spiritual feeling* — that is, *reason-and-feeling in one*. The spiritual feeling is inherently accessible to understanding, which explains why it is self-evident that, besides the action of emotion, the action of intellect becomes prominent in the artist.

Thus the contemporary artist has to work in a double field; or rather, the field of artistic activity, which was formerly vague and diffuse, is now becoming clearly determinate. Although the work of art grows spontaneously, as if *outside him*, the artist has to cultivate the field — before and after growth.

— Piet Mondrian

From a spider's web

The artist is a receptacle for emotions, regardless of whether they spring from heaven, from earth, from a scrap of paper, from a passing face, or from a spider's web.

— Pablo Picasso

Emotion and spirit

Emotion is more outward than spirit. Spirit constructs, compos-es; emotion expresses mood and the like. Spirit constructs most purely, with the simplest line and the most basic color. The more basic the color, the more inward: the more pure.

— Piet Mondrian

Intuitions of the heart

We know truth, not only by the reason, but also by the heart, and it is in this last way that we know first principles; and reason, which has no part in it, tries in vain to impugn them. The skeptics, who have only this for their object, labor to no purpose. We know that we do not dream, and however impossible it is for us to prove it by reason, this inability demonstrates only the weakness of our reason, but not, as they affirm, the uncertainty of all our knowledge. For the knowledge of first principles, as space, time, motion, number, is as sure as any of those which we get from reasoning. And reason must trust these intuitions of the heart, and must base them on every argument. And it is as useless and absurd for reason to demand from the heart proofs of her first principles, before admitting them, as it would be for the heart to demand from reason an intuition of all demonstrated propositions before accepting them.

— Blaise Pascal

The sensation of the mystical

The most beautiful and most profound emotion we can experience is the sensation of the mystical. It is the sower of all true science. He to whom this emotion is a stranger, who can no longer wonder and stand rapt in awe, is as good as dead. To know what is impenetrable to us really exists, manifesting itself as the highest wisdom and the most radiant beauty which our dull faculties can comprehend only in the most primitive form — this knowledge, this feeling is at the center of true religiousness.

— Albert Einstein

EMOTION

The table of my heart

Mine eye hath play'd the painter and hath stell'd
Thy beauty's form in table of my heart;
My body is the frame wherein 'tis held,
And perspective it is best painter's art.
For through the painter must you see his skill
To find where your true image pictur'd lies,
Which in my bosom's shop is hanging still,
That hath his windows glazed with thine eyes.
Now see what good turns eyes for eyes have done:
Mine eyes have drawn thy shape, and thine for me
Are windows to my breast, where through the sun
Delights to peep, to gaze therein on thee;
Yet eyes this cunning want to grace their art:
They draw but what they see, know not the heart.

— William Shakespeare

Emotions acting in unity

Ecstasy is the accurate term for the intensity of consciousness
that occurs in the creative act. But it is not to be thought of
merely as a Bacchic "letting go"; it involves the total person, with
the subconscious and unconscious acting in unity with the conscious. It is not, thus, *irrational*; it is, rather, suprarational. It
brings intellectual, volitional and emotional functions into play
all together.

— Rollo May

Need for passion

Well, in art at any rate you're never on top of the problem. Every stage is simply a step towards the next, not only in the development of the individual artist but in the development also of the general movement to which he is contributing. No form and no color is any use until one makes it one's own — and here's the tricky bit: not only does it have to be one's own but it has also to be a surprise to oneself. It's not patience you need: an unavoidable passion. One can explain patience, but passion cannot be explained. This is what Braque meant when he said about painting that "You can explain everything about it except the bit that matters." If you haven't got that passion, and that inexplicable "bit that matters," you fall into the artist's most dread disease. That disease isn't imitating others — it's imitating oneself. Other people's influence isn't a thing to be frightened of. You've just got to go on feeling that you're a promising young painter who might one day achieve something.

— Ben Nicholson

Begin in health

The creative act . . . is rightly performed only if the artist is healthy, in the sense that he is empty, he is not attached, and everything about him is pure. Then he looks at, and into, this wonderful creation, elicits all the information he needs, and puts everything together in such a way that it makes a good work of art.

— H. H. Shantanand Saraswati

77

SENSES

Quiet attention

This morning I walked into the kitchen and a shaft of light hit the table, it filled the large clay bowl with the four lemons in it. The light from above, the glaze of the earthen bowl reflecting it, and the intense yellow of the lemons radiating it back out. It was like an exquisite prayer. I stood there for a while, folding my own hands into quiet attention.

— Burghild Nina Holzer

Simple observation

So how do you observe a tree, this marvelous thing called a tree, the beauty of it, how do you look at it? . . . Can you watch a tree, or the new moon, or the single star in the heavens, without the word, moon, star, sky — without the word? Because the word is not the actual star, the actual moon. So can you put aside the word and look — that is, look outwardly?

— J. Krishnamurti

A rhythm of all the senses

I found myself putting out an idea that what I am interested in painting is in realizing an experience and not at all in making a painting. It's something to do with creating an enduring reality based on an experience of living which is by no means purely visual but is a rhythm arrived at by means of all the senses. In my work I don't want to achieve a dramatic arresting experience, exciting as that can be, but something more enduring — the kind of thing one finds, say, in the finest Chinese vases or in the Cézanne apple paintings.

— Ben Nicholson

Arriving at a unity of vision

The Right Eye looketh in thee into Eternity. The Left Eye looketh backward in thee into time. If now thou sufferest thyself to be always looking into nature, and the things of time, it will be impossible for thee ever to arrive at the unity, which thou wishest for. . . . Give not thy mind leave to enter in, nor to fill itself with, that which is without thee; neither look thou backward upon thyself . . . . Let not thy Left Eye deceive thee, by making continually one representation after another . . . . And only bringing the Eye of Time into the Eye of Eternity . . . and descending through the Light of God into the Light of Nature . . . shalt thou arrive at the Unity of Vision or Uniformity of Will.

— Jakob Böhme

Direct contact with things

I believe that one thinks much more soundly if the thoughts arise from direct contact with things, than if one looks at things with the aim of finding this or that in them. It is the same with the question of coloring. There are colors which of themselves do beautifully against one another. But I do my best to make it as I see it before I set to work, to do it as I feel it. And yet feeling is a great thing and without it one would not carry out anything. Sometimes I long for harvest time, that is, for the time when I shall be so imbued with the study of nature that I can myself create something in a painting. However, analyzing things is no burden to me nor something I don't like to do.

— Vincent van Gogh

SENSES

Eyes, the receptacles of sensibility

We are attaining a purely expressive art, one that excludes all the styles of the past and is becoming a plastic art with only one purpose: to inspire human nature toward beauty. Light is not a method, it slides toward us, it is communicated to us by our sensibility. Without the perception of light — the eye — there can be no movement. In fact, it is our eyes that transmit the sensations perceived in nature to our soul. Our eyes are the receptacles of the present and, therefore, of our sensibility. Without sensibility, that is, without light, we can do nothing. Consequently, our soul finds its most perfect sensation of life in harmony, and this harmony results only from the simultaneity with which the quantities and conditions of light reach the soul (the supreme sense) by the intermediary of the eyes.

And the soul judges the forms of the image of nature by comparison with nature itself — a pure criticism — and it governs the creator. The creator takes note of everything that exists in the universe through entity, succession, imagination, and simultaneity.

Nature, therefore, engenders the science of painting.

— Robert Delaunay

Senses as a bridge

The senses are our bridge between the incomprehensible and the comprehensible. . . .

— August Macke

Valid seeing

Nature herself reveals little of her secret to those who only look and listen with the outward ear or eye. The condition of all valid seeing, upon every plane of consciousness, lies not in the sharpening of the senses, but in a peculiar attitude of the whole personality: in a self-forgetting attentiveness, a profound concentration, a self-merging, which operates a real communion between the seer and the seen. . . .

— Evelyn Underhill

Raise the gates

We do not commonly live our life out and full; we do not fill all our pores with our blood; we do not inspire and expire fully and entirely enough, so that the wave, the comber, of each inspiration shall break upon our extremest shores, rolling till it meets the sand which bounds us, and the sound of the surf comes back to us. Might not a bellows assist us to breathe? That our breathing should create a wind in a calm day! We live but a fraction of our life. Why do we not let on the flood, raise the gates, and set all our wheels in motion? He that hath ears to hear, let him hear. Employ your senses.

— Henry David Thoureau

82

PART VI

The Nature of the Calling

I did not choose to become an artist; it was decided for me. The inner need for unfoldment, for knowledge and the hard knocks from without, set me on a path I still walk. The path sometimes disappears into the wilderness and I must follow it blindly. I have to search and question and reconsider and let fear destroy my certainty. I am tempered by life; the cauldron of emotions is stirred and I find new strength, new insight. I am transformed and my vision wants a new expression. I am compelled to create a new reality. What an awesome responsibility. I need to take great care in what I set into motion, what I express. I hold the ideal in consciousness and watch the development of the idea fueled by an inner necessity. The imagery and gesture are only the outward forms of the inner meaning, the consciousness through which it manifests. I must tend to my ground of being so as to become a clearer instrument in expressing the joy and freedom that resides in my heart.

There is a lifelong growing; I learn from life, from the wisdom of the ages, from the newest discoveries of science, and I synthesize this input with my intuition. This is my work: to express the ineffable, the mystery of life, and the inner knowledge in a new form.

IDEALS

Heights of exaltation

Inspired by his intuition from this
deep spring of creative essence, man
scales the heights of exaltation in
an ever-expanding endeavor to enlarge
the small portion of space allotted
to him as his share in creation.

— Irene Rice Pereira

Filling a need

I desire not to disgrace the soul. The fact that I am here, certainly shows me that the soul had need of an organ here. Shall I not assume the post? Shall I skulk and dodge and duck with my unseasonable apologies and vain modesty, and imagine my being here impertinent? less pertinent than Epaminondas or Homer being there? and that the soul did not know its own needs? Besides, without any reasoning on the matter, I have no discontent. The good soul nourishes me, and unlocks new magazines of power and enjoyment to me every day. I will not meanly decline the immensity of good, because I have heard that it has come to others in another shape. . . .

— Ralph Waldo Emerson

The highest task

These earnest ones may be informed of my conviction that art is the highest task and the proper metaphysical activity of this life. . . .

— Friedrich Nietzsche

84

IDEALS

To proceed aright

For he who would proceed aright in this matter should begin in youth to visit beautiful forms; and first, if he be guided by his instructor aright, to love one such form only — out of that he should create fair thoughts; and soon he will of himself perceive that the beauty of one form is akin to the beauty of another; and then if beauty of form in general is his pursuit, how foolish would he be not to recognize that the beauty in every form is one and the same! . . . . and he will become a lover of all beautiful forms; in the next stage he will consider that the beauty of the mind is more honorable than the beauty of the outward form . . . . he will go on to the sciences, that he may see their beauty . . . he will create many fair and noble thoughts and notions in boundless love of wisdom; . . . until at last the vision is revealed to him of a single science, which is the science of beauty everywhere. . . .

— Plato

An instrument of the divine melody

I should become the manifestation of the spiritual divine world and an instrument of God's spirit, wherewith he may play upon this sound that I am, as if he were playing upon his own signature: I shall be his instrument and the play of strings of his spoken word and its resonance, and not only I, but all my fellow participants in the magnificently prepared divine instrument. We are all strings in his joyful play of melody; it is the spirit of his mouth that sounds our strings of his voice.

— Jakob Böhme

IDEALS

To serve a noble purpose

It is very important for the artist to gauge his position aright, to realize that he has a duty to his art and to himself, that he is not king of the castle but rather a servant of a nobler purpose. He must search deeply into his own soul, develop and tend it, so that his art has something to clothe, and does not remain a glove without a hand.

The artist must have something to say, for mastery over form is not his goal but rather the adapting of form to its inner meaning.

The artist is not born to a life of pleasure. He must not live idle; he has a hard work to perform, and one which often proves a cross to be borne. He must realize that his every deed, feeling, and thought are raw but sure material from which his work is to arise, that he is free in art but not in life.

— Wassily Kandinsky

Artist as seer

The need of his times works inside the artist without his wanting it, seeing it, or understanding its true significance. In this sense he is close to the seer, the prophet, the mystic. And it is precisely when he does not represent the existing canon but transforms and overturns it that his function rises to the level of the sacral, for he then gives utterance to the authentic and direct revelation of the numinosum.

— Erich Neumann

Towards the positive

What is the use of showing us what is bad without revealing what is good? The Constructive idea prefers that Art perform Positive works which lead us toward the best. The measure of this perfection will not be so difficult to define when we realize that it does not lie outside us but is bound up in our desire and in our will to it. The creative human genius, which never errs and never mistakes, defines this measure. Since the beginning of Time man has been occupied with nothing else but the perfecting of his world.

To find the means for the accomplishment of this task the artist need not search in the external world of Nature; he is able to express his impulses in the language of those absolute forms which are in the substantial possession of his Art.

— Naum Gabo

A global perspective

The student of art, if he is to do more than accumulate facts, must also sacrifice himself: the wider the scope of his study in time and space, the more must he cease to be a provincial, the more he must universalize himself, whatever may be his own temperament and training. He must assimilate whole cultures that seem strange to him, and must also be able to elevate his own levels of reference from those of observation to that of the vision of ideal forms. He must rather love than be curious about the subject of his study. It is just because so much is demanded that the study of "art" can have cultural value, that is to say may become a means of growth. . . .

— Ananda K. Coomaraswamy

IDEALS

Transcending the natural

. . . Only a person who participates in spiritual life has an impulse for a creative activity transcending the merely natural. Otherwise, where would the impulse come from? In all ages the human souls in which the artistic element flourished have had a definite relation to the spiritual world. It was out of a spirit-attuned state that the artistic urge proceeded. And this relation to the spiritual world will be, forever, the prerequisite for genuine creativity.

— Rudolf Steiner

Faith in miracles

The most important tool the artist fashions through constant practice is faith in his ability to produce miracles when they are needed. Pictures must be miraculous: the instant one is completed, the intimacy between the creation and the creator is ended. He is an outsider. The picture must be for him, as for anyone experiencing it later, a revelation, an unexpected and unprecedented resolution of an eternally familiar need.

— Mark Rothko

To pierce the soul

And this it does not seem unreasonable or ungrateful to demand, that the artist should pierce the soul; should command; should not sit aloof & circumambient merely, but should come and take me by the hand and lead me somewhither. . . .

— Ralph Waldo Emerson

Through spiritual knowledge

It is imperative to turn to the spiritual in all spheres. We must make good use of what naturalism has brought us; must not lose what we have acquired by having centuries now held up, as an ideal of art, the imitation of nature. Those who deride materialism are bad artists, bad scientists. Materialism had to happen. We must not look down mockingly on earthly man and the material world. We must have the will to penetrate into this material world spiritually; nor despise the gifts of scientific materialism and naturalistic art; must — though not by developing dry symbolism or allegory — find our way back to the spiritual. . . . We must become artists, not symbolists or allegorists, by rising, through spiritual knowledge, more and more into the spiritual world.

— Rudolf Steiner

Penetrate the world mystery

The present painter is concerned not with his own feelings or with the mystery of his own personality but with the penetration into the world mystery. His imagination is therefore attempting to dig into metaphysical secrets. To that extent his art is concerned with the sublime. It is a religious art which through symbols will catch the basic truth of life. . . . The artist tries to wrest truth from the void. . . .

— Barnett Newman

IDEALS

Pure artistry is eternal

The inner need is built up of three mystical elements: (1) Every artist, as a creator, has something in him which calls for expression (this is the element of personality). (2) Every artist, as child of his age, is impelled to express the spirit of his age (this is the element of style) — dictated by the period and particular country to which the artist belongs (it is doubtful how long the latter distinction will continue to exist). (3) Every artist, as a servant of art, has to help the cause of art (this is the element of pure artistry, which is constant in all ages and among all nationalities).

Only the third element — that of pure artistry — will remain for ever. . . .

. . . The greater the part played in a modern work of art by the two elements of style and personality, the better will it be appreciated by people today; but a modern work of art which is full of the third element will fail to reach the contemporary soul. For many centuries have to pass away before the third element can be received with understanding. But the artist in whose work this third element predominates is the really great artist.

— Wassily Kandinsky

A positive nature

A work of art which inspires us comes from no quibbling or uncertain man. It is the manifest of a very positive nature in great enjoyment, and the very moment the work was done.

— Robert Henri

IDEALS

The pursuit of the sublime

Those who spread their sails in the right way to the winds of the earth will always find themselves borne by a current towards the open seas. The more nobly a man wills and acts, the more avid he becomes for great and sublime aims to pursue. . . . He will want wider organizations to create, new paths to blaze, causes to uphold, truths to discover, an ideal to cherish and defend. . . . The great breath of the universe has insinuated itself into him through the fissure of his humble but faithful action, has broadened him, raised him up, borne him on. . . .

— Teilhard de Chardin

One continuous effort

To be sure, the creative genius of Man is only a part of Nature, but from this part alone derives all the energy necessary to construct his spiritual and material edifice. Being a result of Nature it has every right to be considered as a further cause of its growth. Obedient to Nature, it intends to become its master; attentive to the laws of Nature it intends to make its own laws, following the forms of Nature it re-forms them. We do not need to look for the origin of this activity, it is enough for us to state it and to feel its reality continually acting on us. Life without creative effort is unthinkable, and the whole course of human culture is one continuous effort of the creative will of Man.

— Naum Gabo

PASSION

The love of beauty

What then is the vocation of the whole man? So far as I can make out, his vocation is to be a creator: and if you ask me, Creator of what?, I answer — creator of real values. . . . And if you ask me what motive can be appealed to, what driving power can be relied on, to bring out the creative element in men and women, there is only one answer I can give; but I give it without hesitation — the love of beauty, innate in everybody, but suppressed, smothered, thwarted in most of us. . . .

— L. P. Jacks

To love past reason

If one loves art at all, one must love it beyond all other things in the world, and against such love the reason, if one listened to it, would cry out.

— Oscar Wilde

Seeking artistic truth

The genuine artist, the tradition builder, strives for artistic truth; the other, who obeys merely a blind itch to create, strives for natural resemblance. Through the one, art is brought to its highest peaks, and through the other to its lowest depths.

— Johann Wolfgang von Goethe

Study the unity of nature

A fine balance of spirit with matter can only concur when the artist has so thoroughly submerged himself in the study of the unity of nature as to truly become once more a part of nature — a part of the very earth, thus to view the inner surfaces and the life elements. The material he works with would mean to him more than mere plastic matter, but would act as a coordinant and asset to his theme.

— Isamu Noguchi

Nourished only by life

. . . Imitators, mannerists, start, in art, from the concept; they observe what pleases and affects us in true works of art; understand it clearly, fix it in a concept, and thus abstractly, and then imitate it, openly or disguisedly, with dexterity and intentionally. They suck their nourishment, like parasite plants, from the works of others, and like polypi, they become the color of their food. We might carry comparison further, and say that they are like machines which mince fine and mingle together whatever is put into them, but can never digest it, so that the different constituent parts may always be found again if they are sought out and separated from the mixture; the man of genius alone resembles the organized, assimilating, transforming, and reproducing body. For he is indeed educated and cultured by his predecessors and their works; but he is really fructified only by life and the world directly, through the impression of what he perceives; therefore the highest culture never interferes with his originality.

— Arthur Schopenhauer

PASSION

Clairvoyance

The phenomenal world is merely a means for the artist — just as colors are for the painter, and sounds for the musician — a means for the understanding of the noumenal world and for the expression of that understanding. At the present stage of our development we possess nothing so powerful, as an instrument of knowledge of the world of causes, as art. The mystery of life dwells in the fact that the *noumenon*, i.e., the hidden meaning and the hidden function of a thing, is reflected in its phenomenon . . . . The phenomenon is the image of the noumenon. . . . Only that fine apparatus which is called *the soul of an artist* can understand and feel the reflection of the noumenon in the phenomenon. . . . The artist must be a clairvoyant: he must see that which others do not see; he must be a magician: must possess the power to make others see that which they do not themselves see, but which he does see.

— P. D. Ouspensky

Artist as superman

The ideal artist is he who knows everything, feels everything, experiences everything, and retains his experience in a spirit of wonder and feeds upon it with creative lust. He is therefore best able to select and order the components best suited to fulfill any given desire. The ideal artist is the superman. He uses every possible power, spirit, emotion—conscious or unconscious to arrive at his ends.

— George Bellows

PASSION

The transcendent creative power

My having a definite belief about art also makes me know what I want to get in my own work — and I shall seek to get it even if I myself perish by it.

. . . Sometimes I know so well what I want. In life and in painting too, I can well do without a good Lord, but I cannot, suffering as I am, do without something which is greater than myself, which is my life, the power to create.

— Vincent van Gogh

SELF-DISCOVERY

Conscious spiritual knowledge

I think you too recognize the important relationship between philosophy and art, and it is just this relationship that most painters deny. The great masters do grasp it, unconsciously; but I believe that a painter's conscious spiritual knowledge will have a much greater influence upon his art, and that it would be due only to a weakness in him, or lack of genius, should this spiritual knowledge be harmful to his art. . . .

— Piet Mondrian

The mystical necessity

[The artist's] eyes should be always directed to his own inner life, and his ears turned to the voice of internal necessity. Then he will seize upon all permitted means and just as easily upon all forbidden means. This is the only way of giving expression to mystical necessity.

— Wassily Kandinsky

An explorer

An artist is an explorer. He has to begin by self-discovery and by observation of his own procedure. After that he must not feel under any constraint. But, above all, he must never be too easily satisfied with what he has done. . . .

— Henri Matisse

SELF-DISCOVERY

Divine the inner life

Cézanne made a living thing out of a teacup, or rather in a teacup he realized the existence of something alive. He raised still life to such a point that it ceased to be inanimate.

He painted these things as he painted human beings, because he was endowed with the gift of divining the inner life in everything. His color and form are alike suitable to the spiritual harmony. A man, a tree, an apple, all were used by Cézanne in the creation of something that is called a "picture," and which is a piece of true inward and artistic harmony.

— Wassily Kandinsky

Egoless

I don't express myself in my painting. I express my not-self. The dictum "Know thyself" is only valuable if the ego is removed from the process in search for truth.

— Mark Rothko

The necessity for inner peace

It goes without saying that artists are the most solitary of people — if they view their occupation as a calling. Above and beyond all, an inner peace must pervade their souls and their workshops. If he, the artist, is corrupt, if he is motivated by the market, then the world around him is corrupted. Because he creates the world, he interprets his time and is a symptom of it. If he refuses, he adds to the disorder.

— Julius Bissier

SELF-DISCOVERY

Full stature and proportion

In proportion to his force, the artist will find in his work an outlet for his proper character. He must not be in any manner pinched or hindered by his material, but through his necessity of imparting himself, the adamant will be wax in his hands, and will allow an adequate communication of himself in his full stature and proportion. He need not cumber himself with a conventional nature and culture, nor ask what is the mode in Rome or in Paris. . . .

— Ralph Waldo Emerson

Conscious builder of his ideas

The first and most noble right of the artist is to be a conscious builder of his ideas.

Many highly talented artists of our time bleed to death disregarding their right to work *consciously*. The most honest among them realizes the imperative necessity of new aesthetic laws and the knowledge of these laws.

— Roger Allard

Invent the new being

Today, each artist must undertake to invent himself, a life-long act of creation that constitutes the essential content of the artist's work. The meaning of art in our time flows from this function of self-creation. Art is the laboratory for making new men.

— Harold Rosenberg

SELF-DISCOVERY

Penetrating the surfaces

For an artist to be interesting to us he must have been interesting to himself. He must have been capable of intense feeling, and capable of profound contemplation.

He who has contemplated has met with himself, is in a state to see into the realities beyond the surfaces of his subject.

— Robert Henri

To know in depth

We know something only insofar as we can *express* it — i.e., *make* it. The more complete and multifarious we *produce, create* something, the more we *know* it. We know it completely, when we can *communicate* it, provoke it everywhere, and in every way — effect an individual expression of it in every organ.

— Novalis

Live in the work

It seems to me that the "ultimate intuitions and insights" will only approach one who lives in his work and remains there, and whoever considers them from afar gains no power over them.

— Rainer Maria Rilke

A better and higher self

One should arrive at leading one's conscience to a state of development so that it becomes the voice of a better and a higher self of which the ordinary self is a servant.

— Vincent van Gogh

99

OBEDIENCE

The talent is the call

Each man has his own vocation. The talent is the call. There is one direction in which all space is open to him. He has faculties silently inviting him thither to endless exertion. . . . He inclines to do something which is easy to him, and good when it is done, but which no other man can do. He has no rival. For the more truly he consults his own power, the more difference will his work exhibit from the work of any other. . . .

By doing his work, he makes the need felt which he can supply, and creates the taste by which he is enjoyed. By doing his own work, he unfolds himself. . . .

— Ralph Waldo Emerson

Deep necessities

This is a mystical path. You walk on it daily without knowing what will come tomorrow. But you trust, by writing down the daily fragments of awareness, that a larger network will gradually emerge, that images will come forth, a theme or direction may appear, all of which you could never have outlined, but which emerge out of deep necessities within us.

— Burghild Nina Holzer

Being chosen

People have asked me why I chose to be a dancer. I did not choose. I was chosen to be a dancer, and with that, you live all your life.

— Martha Graham

OBEDIENCE

Your own nature

It is better to do one's own duty, however defective it may be, than to follow the duty of another, however well one may perform it. He who does his duty as his own nature reveals it, never sins.

— The Bhagavad Gita

Sense of direction

Those who fall in love with practice without science are like a sailor who enters a ship without a helm or a compass, and who never can be certain whither he is going. . . .

— Leonardo da Vinci

Faith in the chosen road

I believe that even if I keep on producing work in which one can, if one so desires, . . . point out mistakes, it will have a certain life and a raison d'être of its own which will outdo those faults — in the eye of those who appreciate character and the passings of things through the mind. And with all my faults I cannot be so easily outdone as one would think. I know too well which purpose I am aiming for. I am too firmly convinced that after all I am on the right road — when I want to paint what I feel and feel what I paint — rather than that I bother much about what people say of me.

— Vincent van Gogh

A UNIQUE VOICE

The need to find the ideal

He who cannot find the way to *his* ideal lives more frivolously and shamelessly than the man without an ideal.

— Friedrich Nietzsche

Standing on your own ground

I have not "worked over" the imagery or gimmicks of the past, whether Realist, Surrealist, Expressionist, Bauhaus, Impressionist, or what you choose. I went back to my own idioms, envisioned, created, and thought through. And the insight and the momentum established altered the character of the whole concept of the practice of painting.

— Clyfford Still

Guided by feeling

Be guided by feeling alone. We are only simple mortals, subject to error; so listen to the advice of others, but follow only what you understand and can unite in your own feeling. Be firm, be meek, but follow your own convictions. It is better to be nothing than an echo of other painters. . . . Beauty in art is truth bathed in an impression received from nature. . . . Reality is one part of art; feeling completes it. . . . Before any site and any object, abandon yourself to your first impression. If you have really been touched, you will convey to others the sincerity of your emotion.

— Jean-Baptiste-Camille Corot

A UNIQUE VOICE

Finding a unique expression

I must create a system or be enslaved by another man's;
I will not reason and compare: my business is to create.

— William Blake

Beauty shining through

Once one recognizes that one has the right to be a unique
expression of divinity in humanity; and that the idiosyncrasy of
one's work and life has reason in its wake; that, what might
have been attributed to intuition is consistently underscored by
an original logic; and that the repercussion of that activity has
been generally positive, one can relax into that vein and know
that there is an innate quality of beauty shining through.

— Gilah Yelin Hirsch

The intense life

All art that is worthwhile is a record of intense life, and each
individual artist's work is a record of his special effort, search
and findings, in language especially chosen by himself and
devised best to express him, and the significance of his work
can only be understood by careful study. . . .

— Robert Henri

A UNIQUE VOICE

Finding an authentic voice

Even here, for years I had been a hungry soul, a soldier in the large army of great and small artists, until at last — but better late than never — I have gained consciousness and now I stand hale and hearty before myself. The moment has come for me to write, draw, and paint my credo. In the last month I have destroyed much of my work. . . . Looked at carefully, they were mostly tumors remaining from my bad times. I know them well and the sterner I am with myself the more easily I overcome everything that could hold me back, for I am boiling inside and although artistically I am gladly once again a youth, as we were — do you remember? . . . both excited by a concert . . . was not our excitement then a thing of beauty?

— **Frantisk Kupka**

The long path, alone

It was a journey that one must make, walking straight and alone. No respite or short-cuts were permitted. And one's will had to hold against every challenge of triumph or failure, or the praise of Vanity Fair. Until one had crossed the darkened and wasted valleys and come at last into clear air and could stand on a high limitless plain. Imagination, no longer fettered by the laws of fear, became as one with Vision. And the Act, intrinsic and absolute, was its meaning and the bearer of its passion.

— **Clyfford Still**

The reach of your compassion

I think that art and this knowledge of what art is can be the modern Western way to illumination. It will release you from all kinds of linkages. It will not keep you from practicing all those things you hardly believe in, but it will help you in achieving the esthetic before you become linked to the objects of your life.

When you distinguish between good and evil, you've lost the art. Art goes beyond morality. The reach of your compassion is the reach of your art.

— Joseph Campbell

Remain true to the dream

The artist should fear to become the slave of detail. He should strive to express his thought and not the surface of it. What avails a storm cloud accurate in form and color if the storm is not therein? . . .

It is the first vision that counts. The artist has only to remain true to his dream and it will possess his work in such a manner that it will resemble the work of no other man — for no two visions are alike. . . .

Imitation is not inspiration, and inspiration only can give birth to a work of art. The least of man's original emanation is better than the best of a borrowed thought. . . .

— Albert Pinkham Ryder

Serve the World

Artist as gadfly

Every man who feels in himself the power to create must be a public plague. He must not wait till he is called, he must take no notice when he is dismissed. He must be what Homer praised in his heroes, a gadfly that attacks on one side when driven off from another.

— Johann Wolfang von Goethe

Teach the idea of life

The true artist regards his work as a means of talking with men, of saying his say to himself and to others. It is not a question of pay. . . . The artist is teaching the world the idea of life. The man who believes that money is the thing is cheating himself. The artist teaches that the object of a man's life should be to play as a little child plays. Only it is the play of maturity — the play of one's mental faculties. . . .

— Robert Henri

The heart of the people

I feel my work lies in the heart of the people. . . . I must grasp life in its depths. . . . No result of my work would please me more than that ordinary working people would have such sheets in their rooms or working places. . . .

— Vincent van Gogh

To purify humanity

That the ultimate end of painting is to reach the masses, we have agreed; it is, however, not in the language of the masses that painting should address the masses, but in its own, in order to move, to dominate, to direct, and not in order to be understood. It is the same with religions and philosophies. The artist who abstains from any concessions, who does not explain himself and who tells nothing, builds up an internal strength whose radiance shines all around.

It is in consummating ourselves within ourselves that we shall purify humanity, it is by increasing our own riches that we shall enrich others, it is by setting fire to the heart of the star for our intimate joy that we shall exalt the universe.

— Albert Gleizes & Jean Metzinger

The ultimate goal

Let our artists rather be those who are gifted to discern the true nature of the beautiful and graceful; then will our youth dwell in a land of health, amid fair sights and sounds, and receive the good in everything; and beauty, the effluence of fair works, shall flow into the eye and ear, like a health-giving breeze from a purer region, and insensibly draw the soul from earliest years into likeness and sympathy with the beauty of reason.

— Plato

PART VII

The Ideals of Artistic Expression

*A*rt *by its very nature is not a private pursuit, is not an indulgence of the ego; it reaches out to humanity at large. In fact, it has the power to transform society and the individual. I am elevated by great art. Sacred architecture takes me out of myself into soaring heights; my heart opens when I enter the devotion that hammered the sacred idol. I know bliss in the divinely inspired musical composition; I feel love, the same love the artist felt for his model.*

It is a tall order that art has to fill; at its very best it can create a renaissance, not just of form but of the mind. Art has a mission to hold up the ideal of our human condition. I know what is base in me — greed, misery, loss of heart and courage, the ugly, the vulgar — and I do not wish to be reminded by art of what is base in me.

I know there is an intelligence that imbues this creation with love and beauty, and art in its proper role sings its praises and makes it visible and audible to those who hunger for it.

SOURCES

Universally intelligible

The reference of all production at last to an Aboriginal Power explains the traits common to all works of the highest art, — that they are universally intelligible; that they restore to us the simplest states of mind; and are religious. . . .

— Ralph Waldo Emerson

Sensing the infinite

Art is the *beginning of vision*; it sees vastly more than the most perfect apparatus can discover; and it senses the infinite invisible facets of that crystal, one facet of which we call man.

— P. D. Ouspensky

The eternal bearing witness

The work of art expresses precisely those things which do not die. It must do so, however, in a form that bears witness to the artist's own era.

—Constantin Brancusi

Expressing the inexpressible

In art only one thing matters: that which cannot be explained.

— Georges Braque

Toward the imaginative depth

A painting carries within itself its *raison d'être*. You may take it with impunity from a church to a drawing-room, from a museum to a study. Essentially independent, necessarily complete, it need not immediately satisfy the mind: on the contrary, it should lead it, little by little, toward the imaginative depths where burns the light of organization. It does not harmonize with this or that ensemble, it harmonizes with the totality of things, with the universe: it is an organism.

— Albert Gleizes and Jean Metzinger

The lofty mission

There is no loftier mission than to approach the Godhead more nearly than other mortals and by means of that contact to spread the rays of the Godhead through the human race.

— Ludwig van Beethoven

111

The world without art

Without poets, without artists, men would soon weary of nature's monotony. The sublime idea men have of the universe would collapse with dizzying speed. The order which we find in nature, and which is only an effect of art, would at once vanish. Everything would break up in chaos. There would be no season, no civilizations, no thought, no humanity; even life would give way, and the impotent void would reign everywhere.

— Guillaume Apollinaire

The bond of art and soul

Painting is an art, and art is not vague production, transitory and isolated, but a power which must be directed to the improvement and refinement of the human soul — to, in fact, the raising of the spiritual triangle. . . .

. . . When the human soul is gaining greater strength, art will also grow in power, for the two are inextricably connected and complementary one to the other. Conversely, at those times when the soul tends to be choked by material disbelief, art becomes purposeless and talk is heard that art exists for art's sake alone. Then is the bond between art and the soul, as it were, drugged into unconsciousness. The artist and the spectator drift apart, till finally the latter turns his back on the former or regards him as a juggler whose skill and dexterity are worthy of applause.

— Wassily Kandinsky

Reflecting spiritual prototypes

In order to understand [Buddhist art] one must be not merely a sensitive man, but also a spiritual man; and not merely a spiritual, but also a sensitive man. One must have learned that an access to reality cannot be had by making a choice between matter and spirit considered as things unlike in all respects, but rather by seeing in things material and sensible a formal likeness to spiritual prototypes of which the senses can give no direct report. It is not a question of religion versus science, but of a reality on different levels of reference, or better, perhaps, of different orders of reality, not mutually exclusive.

— Ananda K. Coomaraswamy

The interior splendor

The art which only gilds the surface and demands merely a superficial polish, without reaching to the core is but varnish and filigree. But the work of genius is rough-hewn from the first, because it anticipates the lapse of time and has an ingrained polish, which still appears when fragments are broken off, an essential quality of its substance. Its beauty is its strength. It breaks with a luster, and splits in cubes and diamonds. Like the diamond, it has only to be cut to be polished, and its surface is a window to its interior splendors.

— Henry David Thoreau

HIGHEST IDEALS

Toward universal inwardness

A true conception of the *essential meaning* of spirit and nature in man shows life and art as a perpetual sacrifice of inward to outward and outward to inward, a conception that enables us to recognize this process as exclusively in favor of the inward and *serving to broaden man's individual inwardness (spirit) toward universal inwardness.*

Thus understood, the opposition of spirit and nature in man is seen as constantly forming a *new unity* — which *constantly reflects more purely* the original unity out of which the opposites, spirit and nature, manifest themselves — in time — as a duality.

Pure vision shows us this original unity as the *enduring force* in all things, as the *universally shared force common to all things.*

— Piet Mondrian

Seeking the spirit

The task of art is to take hold of the shining, the radiance, the manifestation, of that which as spirit weaves and lives throughout the world. All genuine art seeks the spirit. Even when art wishes to represent the ugly, the disagreeable, it is concerned, not with the sensory-disagreeable as such, but with the spiritual which proclaims its nature in the midst of unpleasantness. If the spiritual shines through the ugly, even the ugly becomes beautiful. In art it is upon a relation to the spiritual that beauty depends.

— Rudolf Steiner

Harmony

Harmony full and free in Mondrian's work — The idea is one — the expression is one — The color is one with the directions — the values are one with the scale — the even flatness is one with the profundity — each element is in its utter purity — utterly different from anything else in the realm of thought — that utter purity is its harmony — harmony is its essential nature and the Truth at the back of Reality — Harmony is not conformity — Balance is not equipoise between two equal forces, neutralizing one another — What Harmony in its utter purity is — you cannot state — words are facets not the Whole — but you can experience it — if you are lucky once or twice in a lifetime. . . . All men can experience it in the presence of Love — and in the presence of Healing — great healing from the proximity of death — and those of us who have trained our eyes to see not things but living forces — can experience it in the presence of Beauty. Such beauty is the harmony of Mondrian's work — and it I cannot state, but I have wondered before it, seen it — I can note a few truths that I have observed about it — round white pebbles that others may recognize as landmarks along this road — if they travel that way too —this road which has no end — these are a few of them.

— Winifred Nicholson

HIGHEST IDEALS

The perennial wisdom

Far from the cliché that people have formed of the artist, with all its onus of originality, personality, style, etc., that allows the work to speak in the outside world, for the author there is, above all, a core of more anonymous thought, of collective thought, of which he is no more than the modest servant. This is surely the area where the wisdom that underlies all the ideologies and fateful contingencies of the world must be stored. It is the impulse of our instinct to live, to know, to love, to be free that has been preserved and revived by the perennial wisdom. The ways in which it becomes definite, which cannot be ignored if its messages are to be understood, are the necessary episodes of the very laws of growth that art displays in any given moment.

— Antoni Tàpies

Superfluity; beyond necessity

The mother of the useful arts is necessity; that of the fine arts superfluity. As their father, the former have understanding; the latter genius, which is itself a kind of superfluity, that of the powers of knowledge beyond the measure which is required for the service of the will.

— Arthur Schopenhauer

Relation to cosmic law

Abstract painting leaves behind the "skin" of nature, but not its laws. Let me use the "big words" *cosmic laws*. Art can only be great if it relates directly to cosmic laws and is subordinated to them.

— Wassily Kandinsky

Harmony with universal law

The purpose of engineering is TO CREATE STRUCTURES; the purpose of architecture is TO CREATE EMOTIONS. Architectural emotion arises when a work strikes a chord within us that harmonizes with universal laws we recognize, submit to, and admire. When certain proportions are established, the work takes hold of us. Architecture is proportion — a pure creation of the mind.

— Le Corbusier

The soul's free moving

Painting is an art which man can experience inwardly. Whether he creates as a painter or just lives in and enjoys a painting, it is a soul event. . . . Really, what is experienced in painting — despite the imperfections of pigments — is the soul's free moving about in the cosmos.

— Rudolf Steiner

Toward the universal

Subjectivization of the universal in art lowers the universal on the one hand, while on the other it makes possible the rise of the individual toward the universal.

Subjectivization of the universal — the work of art — can express the consciousness of an age either in its relationship *to the universal*, or its relationship to *daily life*, to the *individual*. In the first case, art is *truly religious*, in the second *profane*. A high degree of the universal in the consciousness of an age, even if it is spontaneous intuition, can elevate its art above the common-place; but *truly religious art* already transcends it by its very nature. For the universal — although its germ is already in us — towers far above us; and just as far above us is that art which directly expresses the universal. Such an art, like religion, is united with life at the same time as it transcends (ordinary) life.

—Piet Mondrian

The highest kind of justice

Any work that aspires, however humbly, to the condition of art should carry its justification in every line.

Art itself may be defined as a single-minded attempt to render the highest kind of justice to the visible universe, by bringing to light the truth, manifold and one, underlying its every aspect.

— Joseph Conrad

The experience of time

Where the artist is not concerned with quantitative measure-
ment of time but with the quality of his experience of an
event's duration in his consciousness, a lifetime's duration may
shorten to nothing, and a moment's experience may have a
span of time lasting without end and having no beginning. . . .

The rhythm of the duration of an event is an experience of our
consciousness whose beginning and end is not determined by
the clock but by its duration within our consciousness, and
once there, it has no other dimensions and no other limits save
the limits of the experience itself. Time becomes, in that case, a
part of our consciousness where minutes and seconds and days
and years have no meaning. It is a presence without intervals,
since in our consciousness the intervals themselves are events
and are experienced by their duration.

An artist, in making an image of his experience of an event, has to
bring this experience of time into it if he wants the image to convey the experience of life in that event . . . . to carry the experience
of its happening to the spectator in the image he is creating of it.

— Naum Gabo

The holographic view

. . . A work of art is the same as any perfect organism. It is so
homogeneous in its composition that it reveals its true inner
essence in each detail. If you cut any part of the human body, the
same blood will flow. If you hear one verse of a poem, one measure of a piece of music, you are able to comprehend the whole.

— Arnold Schönberg

119

UNIVERSAL PRINCIPLES

The Three Plastic Virtues: Purity, unity, and truth

The three plastic virtues, purity, unity, and truth, stand triumphantly over vanquished nature. . . .

Fire is the symbol of painting, and the three plastic virtues are aflame and radiant.

Fire has the purity that suffers the existence of nothing foreign to itself and cruelly transforms into itself whatever it touches.

It has that magic unity which means that if it is divided, each particle will be like the single flame.

Finally, it has the sublime truth of its light, which no one can deny. . . .

Purity is the forgetfulness that comes after study. For a pure artist to die, all those of past centuries would have had not to exist. . . .

To esteem purity is to baptize one's instincts, humanize art, and exalt the personality. . . .

But the painter must above all be aware of his own divinity, and the paintings he offers up to the admiration of other men will confer on them the glory of experiencing also, for a moment, their own divinity.

To do that, one must take in at a single glance the past, the present, and the future.

The painting must present that essential unity which alone produces ecstasy. . . .

The painting will exist ineluctably. The vision will be whole, complete; its infinity, instead of signaling an imperfection, will only accentuate the relationship of a new creature to a new creator, and nothing else. Otherwise, there will be no unity, and the relationships that will exist between various points on the canvas and various essences, objects, and kinds of light will produce only a multiplicity of disparate and unharmonious parts. . . .

Purity and unity do not count without truth, which cannot be compared to reality since it is the same, outside all the natures that attempt to retain us in the fatal order in which we are but animals.

Above all, artists are men who want to become inhuman.

They are painfully looking for the trail of inhumanity, a trail one finds nowhere in nature.

That trail is the truth, and outside of it, we recognize no reality.

But reality will never be discovered once and for all, truth will always be new.

— Guillaume Apollinaire

An immediate force

The force of Art lies in its immediate influence on human psychology and in its active contagiousness. Being a creation of Man it re-creates Man. Art has no need of philosophical arguments, it does not follow the signposts of philosophical systems; Art, like life, dictates systems to philosophy. It is not concerned with the meditation about what is and how it came to be. That is a task for Knowledge. Knowledge is born of the desire to know, Art derives from the necessity to communicate and to announce.

— Naum Gabo

121

Idea, a living organism

The *Idea* is the unity that falls into multiplicity on account of the temporal and spatial form of our intuitive apprehension; the *concept*, on the contrary, is the unity reconstructed out of multiplicity by the abstraction of our reason . . . . The *concept* is like a dead receptacle, in which whatever has been put actually lies side by side, but out of which no more can be taken (by analytical judgment) than was put in (by synthetical reflection); the (Platonic) *Idea*, on the other hand, develops, in him who has comprehended it, ideas which are new as regards the concept of the same name; it resembles a living organism, developing itself and possessed of the power of reproduction, which brings forth what was not put into it.

It follows from all that has been said, that the concept . . . necessary and productive as it is in science, yet [is] always barren and unfruitful in art. The comprehended Idea, on the contrary, is the true and only source of every work of art. In its powerful originality it is only derived from life itself, from nature, from the world, and that only by the true genius, or by him whose momentary inspiration reaches the point of genius. Genuine and immortal works of art spring only from such direct apprehension.

— Arthur Schopenhauer

Matter worked by mind

The rendering of reality existing and remaining outside of us is not art. It has not and cannot have any value as art. It is not and cannot be anything more than a blind imitation of nature and therefore a mere material reproduction. Matter must be worked on by the mind to attain lasting form.

— Giovanni Segantini

Fusion of sensibility and power

When Acton said "All power corrupts and absolute power corrupts absolutely," this is only a partial truth, but if the destructive element in power alone is married to an equally "powerful" sensibility only then indeed it becomes a constructive force. The deepest works of art are possibly those which combine an element of this deep feminine sensibility with an equally deep masculine power: neither can create without the other. A civilization can be gauged by the degree of equality reached between man and woman.

— Ben Nicholson

A fairer creation than we know

Because the soul is progressive, it never quite repeats itself, but in every act attempts the production of a new and fairer whole. . . . Thus in our fine arts, not imitation, but creation is the aim. In landscapes, the painter should give the suggestion of a fairer creation than we know. The details, the prose of nature he should omit, and give us only the spirit and splendor. . . . In a portrait, he must inscribe the character, and not the features, and must esteem the man who sits to him as himself only an imperfect picture or likeness of the aspiring original within.

— Ralph Waldo Emerson

UNIVERSAL PRINCIPLES

Free movement of genius

In art the best of all is too spiritual to be given directly to the senses; it must be born in the imagination of the beholder, although begotten by the work of art. It depends upon this that the sketches of great masters often effect more than their finished pictures; although another advantage certainly contributes to this, namely, that they are completed offhand in the moment of conception; while the perfected painting is only produced through continued effort, by means of skillful deliberation and persistent intention, for the inspiration cannot last till it is completed. . . . Certainly the artist ought to think in the arranging of his work; but only that thought which was *perceived* before it was thought has afterward, in its communication, the power of animating and rousing, and thereby becomes imperishable. . . . The work which is done at a stroke . . . the work which is completed in the inspiration of its first conception, and as it were unconsciously dashed off . . . . [these] have the great advantage of being purely the work of the ecstasy of the moment, the inspiration, the free movement of genius, without any admixture of intention and reflection; hence they are through and through delightful and enjoyable, without shell and kernel, and their effect is much more inevitable than that of the greatest works of art, of slower and more deliberate execution.

— Arthur Schopenhauer

Alive and moving

Beauty must come back to the useful arts, and the distinction between the fine and the useful arts be forgotten. . . . In nature, all is useful, all is beautiful. It is therefore beautiful, because it is alive, moving, reproductive; it is therefore useful, because it is symmetrical and fair. Beauty will not come at the call of a legislature, nor will it repeat in England or America its history in Greece. It will come, as always, unannounced, and spring up between the feet of brave and earnest men.

— Ralph Waldo Emerson

The restored original of nature

The true art is not merely a sublime consolation and holiday labor which the gods have given to sickly mortals, to be wrought at in parlors, and not in stithies amid soot and smoke, but such a masterpiece as you may imagine a dweller on the table-lands of Central Asia might produce, with threescore and ten years for canvas, and the faculties of a man for tools — a human life, wherein you might hope to discover more than the freshness of Guido's Aurora, or the mild light of Titian's landscapes, not a bald imitation or rival of Nature, but the restored original of which she is the reflection.

— Henry David Thoreau

Elevating the Human Spirit

Others, too, will love

. . .

Prophets of Nature, we to them will speak
A lasting inspiration, sanctified
By reason, blest by faith: what we have loved,
Others will love, and we will teach them how;
Instruct them how the mind of man becomes
A thousand times more beautiful than the earth
On which he dwells, above this frame of things
(Which, 'mid all revolution in the hopes
And fears of men, doth still remain unchanged)
In beauty exalted, as it is itself
Of quality and fabric more divine.

— **William Wordsworth**

Cultivating the spirit

If drawing proceeds from the Spirit and color from the senses, one must draw in order to cultivate the Spirit and to be capable of guiding color into the paths of the Spirit. . . .

— Henri Matisse

Re-educating vision

There are those who say that one of the goals of art is to challenge. I prefer to reframe that as re-educating vision. If the end is to stimulate harmony and beauty through thoughtful evocation of the mind and senses, then that is a meaningful challenge.

— **Gilah Yelin Hirsch**

To educate the perception

Thus, historically viewed, it has been the office of art to educate the perception of beauty. We are immersed in beauty, but our eyes have no clear vision. It needs, by the exhibition of single traits, to assist and lead the dormant taste. We carve and paint, or we behold what is carved and painted, as students of the mystery of Form. The virtue of art lies in detachment, in sequestering one object from the embarrassing variety. Until one thing comes out from the connection of things, there can be enjoyment, contemplation, but no thought . . . . . The power depends on the depth of the artist's insight of that object he contemplates. For every object has its roots in central nature, and may of course be so exhibited to us as to represent the world. . . .

— Ralph Waldo Emerson

Inviting the viewer

Anything is possible! For everything takes place in a field infinitely larger than that which delimits the size of the painting or grander than that which appears physically in the painting. The painting is simply a "support" that invites the viewer to participate in the much broader game of a thousand and one visions and feelings. It is the talisman that builds or tears down walls in the deepest corners of our spirit, that opens, and sometimes closes, the doors and windows in the constructions of our impotence, our slavery, or our freedom.

— Antoni Tàpies

ELEVATING THE HUMAN SPIRIT

Teaching contemplation

Only a work of art teaches true contemplation: all the great events and actions of our own time only excite our hate or love, our sympathy or dislike, our approval or censure. Only in the mirror of art can we find true contemplation, calmness, and support.

— Johann Wolfgang von Goethe

Food for enjoyment

The eye seeks to refresh itself through your work; give it food for enjoyment, not dejection. . . . Let everything about you breathe the calm and peace of the soul. . . .

— Paul Gauguin

A baptism of mind and soul

A work of art is only truly such in so far as originating in the human spirit, it continues to belong to the soil from which it sprang, has received, in short, the baptism of the mind and soul of man, and only presents that which is fashioned in consonance with such a sacrament. An interest vital to man, the spiritual values which the single event, one individual character, one action possesses in its devolution and final issue, is seized in the work of art and emphasized with greater purity and clarity than is possible on the ground of ordinary reality where human art is not. And for this reason the work of art is of higher rank than any product of Nature whatever, which has not submitted to this passage through the mind.

— G. W. F. Hegel

The internal truth of art

If the emotional power of the artist can overwhelm the "how?" and can give free scope to his finer feelings, then art is on the crest of the road by which she will not fail later on to find the "what" she has lost, the "what" which will show the way to the spiritual food of the newly awakened spiritual life. This "what?" will no longer be the material, objective "what" of the former period, but the internal truth of art, the soul without which the body (i.e., the "how") can never be healthy, whether in an individual or in whole people.

This "what" is the internal truth which only art can divine, which only art can express by those means of expression which are hers alone.

— Wassily Kandinsky

An effort of consciousness

To be constructive means to me precisely to be guided by the pattern of our consciousness and to create our images according to the structure of our consciousness itself, for only in this way shall we be able to fulfill the task of keeping the state of mind of the human being, including our own, in balance and in harmony with the laws of life, thus enhancing its growth.

. . . Art is an effort of our consciousness directed toward a specific goal — to know and to make known, to give shape to the shapeless, structure to the discomposed, and to lend form to the amorphous origin of chaos.

— Naum Gabo

The quality of character

But there does exist, none the less, an absolute standard of artistic merit. And it is a standard which is in the last resort a moral one. Whether a work of art is good or bad depends entirely on the quality of the character which expresses itself in the work. Not that all virtuous men are good artists, nor all artists conventionally virtuous . . . . That virtue is the virtue of integrity, of honesty towards oneself. Bad art is of two sorts: that which is merely dull, stupid, and incompetent, the negatively bad; and the positively bad, which is a lie and a sham. Very often the lie is so well told that almost everyone is taken in by it — for a time. In the end, however, lies are always found out.

— Aldous Huxley

Inner life guarantees truth

. . . Serious art has been the work of individual artists whose art has had nothing to do with "style" because they were not in the least connected with the style or the needs of the masses. Their works arose rather in defiance of their times. They are characteristic, fiery signs of a new era that increase daily everywhere. . . . . What appears spectral today will be natural tomorrow.

Where are such signs and works? How do we recognize the genuine ones?

Like everything genuine, its inner life guarantees its truth. All works of art created by truthful minds without regard for the work's conventional exterior remain genuine for all times.

— Franz Marc

Evolution of culture

Culture is an accrued pattern of creation in form, and participation in events which generally give feelings of joy, health, and catharsis to the individual, family, and community. After much repetition, eventually called ritual, tradition is noticed. Only after centuries of remembering and experimenting is a palpable edifice called culture evolved.

— Gilah Yelin Hirsch

Bridging the abyss

Fortunately the abyss on the edge of which man lives, the abyss opening out before him in religion and cognition, can be bridged. But not by contemporary religion, nor yet by a cognition, a science, derived wholly from the earth.

It is here that art enters. It forms a bridge across the abyss. That is why art must realize that its task is to carry the spiritual–divine life into the earthly; to fashion the latter in such a way that its forms, colors, words, tones, act as a revelation of the world beyond. Whether art takes on an idealistic or realistic coloring is of no importance. What it needs is a relationship to the truly, not merely thought-out, spiritual.

— Rudolf Steiner

Transforming Life and Society

A pure expression of the age

If art is to be a *living reality* for modern man, it has to be a pure expression of the new consciousness of that age. Art can become a living reality for him if and only if by contemplation he can become one with the universality it expresses; (In this way abstract-real painting can also be art even for those in whom the modern spirit is not yet determinate, for its spiritual content can be unconsciously *felt*) but art has yet to become one with his *whole being*.

— Piet Mondrian

Union of kindred spirits

Nothing is more hallowing than the union of kindred spirits in art. At the moment of meeting, the art lover transcends himself. At once he is and is not. He catches a glimpse of Infinity, but words cannot voice his delight, for the eye has no tongue. Freed from the fetters of matter, his spirit moves in the rhythm of things. It is thus that art becomes akin to religion and ennobles mankind. It is this which makes a masterpiece something sacred. . . .

— Kakuzo Okakura

To the heart of people

When a man of good being takes to experience and expression, then art manifests and it goes straight to the heart of people. Rules are not what matter most; it is being and experience that matter.

— H. H. Shantanand Saraswati

The genius of the hour

But the artist must employ the symbols in use in his day and nation, to convey his enlarged sense to his fellow-men. Thus the new in art is always formed out of the old. The Genius of the Hour sets his ineffaceable seal on the work, and gives it an inexpressible charm for the imagination. As far as the spiritual character of the period overpowers the artist, and finds expression in his work, so far it will retain a certain grandeur, and will represent to future beholders the Unknown, the Inevitable, the Divine.

— Ralph Waldo Emerson

Living, fully living

Art, always a daughter of the divine, has become estranged from her parent. If it finds its way back to its origins and is again accepted by the divine, then it will become what it should within civilization, within world-wide culture: a boon for mankind. . . .

The need is not for theory — art is not theory. The need is for living, fully living, in the artistic quality while striving for understanding. Such an orientation leads beyond discussion to genuine appreciation and creation.

— Rudolf Steiner

The ideals of a nation

Fine art is not art in the true sense of the term until it is also thus free, and its *highest* function is only then satisfied when it has established itself in a sphere which it shares with religion and philosophy, becoming thereby merely one mode and form through which the *Divine*, the profoundest interest of mankind, and spiritual truths of widest range, are brought home to consciousness and expressed. It is in works of art that nations have deposited the richest intuitions and ideas they possess.

— G. W. F. Hegel

A deeper understanding of life

True art does not have to make itself clear: it is always clear by its very nature. But this is not perceived by the multitude.

Because the expression of art is always changing, only an elite understands its continuous evolution. Through this elite, true aesthetic culture is formed. The multitude are conservative: they do nothing but impede evolution, while following it from a distance.

The artist is concerned neither with the elite nor with the multitude: he follows his intuition, which, through the progress of life, becomes more and more clear — so clear that it is usually confused with intellect. Only in this way can the artist gradually raise the multitude to a deeper and deeper understanding of life.

— Piet Mondrian

Choice in creation

The goal of the conscious and conscientious individual and community is self-renewal through self-creation. Choice forms the basis of creation, whether it be behavioral or aesthetic. Any creation must be undertaken with a profound understanding of the relation of causality to repercussive events in the short and long run. With an eye to the future, humanity can reassess the actions of the past and change the direction of the present. With intelligence and foresight, goals can be redirected and refined.

— Gilah Yelin Hirsch

Awaken the beholder

Art has not yet come to its maturity, if it do not put itself abreast with the most potent influences of the world, if it is not practical and moral, if it do not stand in connection with the conscience, if it do not make the poor and uncultivated feel that it addresses them with a voice of lofty cheer. There is higher work for Art than the arts. . . . Art is the need to create; but in its essence, immense and universal, it is impatient of working with lame or tied hands, and of making cripples and monsters, such as all pictures and statues are. Nothing less than the creation of man and nature is its end. A man should find in it an outlet for his whole energy. He may paint and carve only as long as he can do that. Art should exhilarate, and throw down the walls of circumstance on every side, awakening in the beholder the same sense of universal relation and power which the work evinced in the artist, and its highest effect is to make new artists.

— Ralph Waldo Emerson

Balance, purity, and serenity

I cannot copy nature in a servile way, I must interpret nature and submit it to the spirit of the picture — when I have found the relationship of all the tones, the result must be a living harmony of tones, a harmony not unlike that of a musical composition. . . .

What I dream of is an art of balance, of purity and serenity devoid of troubling or depressing subject-matter, an art which might be for every mental worker, be he businessman or writer, like an appeasing influence, like a mental soother, something like a good armchair in which to rest from physical fatigue.

— Henri Matisse

A real transaction

If I must place my trust somewhere, I would invest it in the psyche of sensitive observers who are free of the conventions of understanding. I would have no apprehensions about the use they would make of the pictures for the needs of their own spirit. For if there is both need and spirit, there is bound to be a real transaction.

— Mark Rothko

Sharing the joy of creation

The act of creation and the act of appreciation of beauty are not, in essence, distinguishable. . . . In the actual moment of appreciation, . . . the beholder experiences those precise emotions which passed through the mind of the creator in his moment of creation. With the help of the artist he himself shares the joy of creation. . . .

— H. E. Huntley

TRANSFORMING LIFE AND SOCIETY

A new awareness

It is a proven fact that works of art have an influence on people. I endeavor to make a picture, for instance, exert a positive influence on the observer by its coloring, mood, and compositional idea, encouraging, say, activation, tranquilization, concentration, or harmony; a culture should evoke a new awareness of space and volume, new knowledge and emotions.

— Max Bill

A refining influence

Art in the community has a subtle, unconscious, refining influence.

It practically means that the presence of good art will unconsciously refine a community and that poor art will do it incalculable harm.

— Robert Henri

A communion of minds

The sympathetic communion of minds necessary for art appreciation must be based on mutual concession. The spectator must cultivate the proper attitude for receiving the message, as the artist must know how to impart it. The tea-master, Kobori Enshiu, himself a daimyo, has left to us these memorable words: "Approach a great painting as thou wouldst approach a great prince." In order to understand a masterpiece, you must lay yourself low before it and await with bated breath its least utterance.

— Kakuzo Okakura

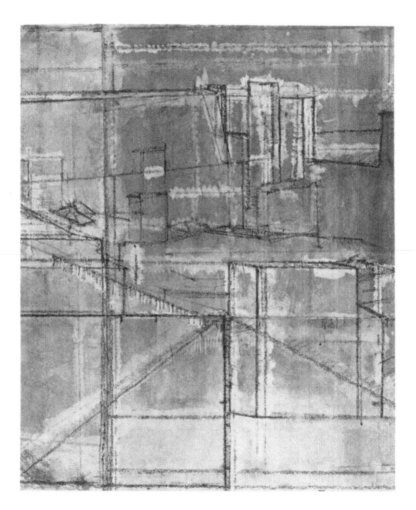

Part VIII

Infinite Forms of Expression

The infinite variety of expressing through art the ground of our being, an abstract idea, or human emotion is the very proof of the infinite potential of the Creative Principle. I marvel at the poetic beauty of the hymns from the Rig-Veda. Compiled five thousand years ago by the great seers, it is a song of praise to the cosmic powers. The meaning is universal; it transcends time and has the power to open the heart and raise the consciousness.

I look to primal forms for inspiration and reflect on the intricate geometric relationships of the Platonic Solids. The Golden Mean, that mysterious Phi proportion used in painting, sculpture, and architecture, is at the very heart of creation and gives endless potential for growth and regeneration.

Form is expressive; when it is harmonious, it speaks to the harmony within. Color and sound speak directly to the emotions. Form and line, based on number and measure, speak directly to the mind. The more universal, the more primal the thought and form, the more powerfully it will speak. It will stand clear and comprehensible, aloof of mannerisms, style, and method.

IDEALS

The forming power

Here then, said [Theocles], is all I would have explained to you before. "That the beautiful, the fair, the comely, were never in the matter, but in the art and design; never in body itself, but in the form or forming power." Does not the beautiful form confess this, and speak the beauty of the design whenever it strikes you? What is it but the design which strikes? What is it you admire but mind, or the effect of mind? 'Tis mind alone which forms. All which is void of mind is horrid, and matter formless is deformity itself.

— Shaftesbury

The mystery of form

Form is a mystery to us for it is the expression of mysterious powers. Only through it do we sense the secret powers, the "invisible God."

— August Macke

Freedom and style

An iconography may not vary for millennia, and yet the style of every century will be distinct and recognizable at a glance. It is in this respect that the intellectual operation is called free; the style is the man, and that in which the style of one individual or period differs from that of another is the infallible trace of the artist's personal nature; not a deliberate, but an unconscious self-expression of the free man.

— Ananda K. Coomaraswamy

Spirit in the work

There is no such thing as architecture. There is the spirit of architecture, but it has no presence. What does have presence is a work of architecture. At best it must be considered as an offering to architecture itself, merely because of the wonder of its beginning.

— Louis I. Kahn

Plato's intelligible form

We begin to see now why primitive and traditional and what we have described as normal art is "abstract"; it is an imitation, not of a visible and transient appearance or "effect of light," but of an intelligible form which need no more resemble any natural object than a mathematical equation need look like its locus in order to be "true." It is one thing to draw in linear rhythms and abstract light because one must; another thing for anyone who is not by nature and in the philosophical sense a realist, deliberately to cultivate an abstracted style.

— Ananda K. Coomaraswamy

Find the natural unity

Good taste is not in making the right choice, but in perceiving in something the natural unity between its quantities and qualities. . . .

— Kahlil Gibran

Harmonic Proportion

Harmony is sensibility ordered by the creator, who must try to render the greatest degree of realistic expression, or what might be called the subject; the Subject is harmonic proportion, and this proportion is composed of various simultaneous elements in a single action. The subject is eternal in the work of art, and it must be apparent to the initiated in all its order, all its science.

Without the subject, there are no possibilities. This does not, however, mean a literary and, therefore, anecdotal subject; the subject of painting is exclusively plastic, and it results from vision. It must be the pure expression of human nature.

The eternal subject is to be found in nature itself; the inspiration and clear vision characteristic of the wise man, who discovers the most beautiful and powerful boundaries.

— Robert Delaunay

Detail serves the whole

A painter, if he has any genius, understands the truth and unity of design; and knows he is even then unnatural when he follows Nature too close, and strictly copies Life. For his art allows him not to bring all nature into his piece, but a part only. However, his piece, if it be beautiful, and carries truth, must be a whole, by itself, complete, independent, and withal as great and comprehensive as he can make it. So that particulars, on this occasion, must yield to the general design, and all things be subservient to that which is principal; in order to form a certain easiness of sight, a simple, clear, and united view. . . .

— Shaftesbury

The depth of the human form

What interests me most is neither still life nor landscape but the human figure. It is through it that I best succeed in expressing the nearly religious feeling that I have towards life. I do not insist upon the details of the face. I do not care to repeat them with anatomical exactness. Though I happen to have an Italian model whose appearance at first suggests nothing but a purely animal existence, yet I succeed in picking out among the lines of his face those which suggest that deep gravity which persists in every human being. A work of art must carry in itself its complete significance and impose it upon the beholder even before he can identify the subject matter.

— Henri Matisse

Primacy of forms

On shapes:

They are unique elements in a unique situation.

They are organisms with volition and a passion for self-assertion.

They move with internal freedom, and without need to conform with or to violate what is probable in the familiar world.

They have no direct association with any particular visible experience, but in them one recognizes the principle and passion of organisms.

— Mark Rothko

MODES

Lines and colors speaking

It is surprising to me how many people separate the objective from the abstract. Objective painting is not good painting unless it is good in the abstract sense. A hill or tree cannot make a good painting just because it is a hill or a tree. It is lines and colors put together so that they say something. For me that is the very basis of painting. The abstraction is often the most definite form for the intangible thing in myself that I can only clarify in paint.

— Georgia O'Keeffe

Conscious created beauty

Naturalistic beauty is now purified and returns to its origin: "pure intuition." Created beauty is no longer vague and imitative, but conscious and creative. It is sometimes at variance with cerebral logic but always in accord with pure logic. Hence this uninhibited power, this clear new beauty which shows the universal as equivalent with the individual.

Well executed, works of purely abstract art will always remain fully human, not "although" but precisely "because" their appearance is not a naturalistic one.

— Piet Mondrian

The choice sensation

The great artist has not reproduced nature, but has expressed by his extract the most choice sensation it has made upon him.

— Robert Henri

Abstract versus figurative

There is no abstract art. You must always start with something. Afterwards you can remove all traces of reality. There's no danger then, anyway, because the idea of the object will have left an indelible mark. It is what started the artist off, excited his ideas, and stirred up his emotions. Ideas and emotions will in the end be prisoners in his work. . . .

Nor is there any "figurative" and "non-figurative" art. Everything appears to us in the guise of a "figure." Even in metaphysics ideas are expressed by means of symbolic "figures.". . . See how ridiculous it is, then, to think of painting without "figuration."

— Pablo Picasso

The vibrations of color

Abstract art is a beginning towards freeing the old pictorial formula. But the real new painting will begin when people understand that color has a life of its own, that the infinite combinations of color have a poetry and a language much more expressive than the old methods. It is a mysterious language in tune with the vibrations, the life itself, of color. In this area, there are new and infinite possibilities.

— Sonia Delaunay

Simplicity

Simplicity is not a goal in art, but one arrives at simplicity in spite of oneself by approaching the real sense of things.

— Constantin Brancusi

145

MODES

Number as source

NUMBER IS THE FORMAL POWER
of the continuum;
the root and source of the
eternal ever-coming "To Be";
and the never-ceasing abundance
                    of creative FORMS.

— Irene Rice Pereira

Geometry and poetic idea

The geometrical forms often used by abstract artists do not
indicate, as has been thought, a conscious and intellectual
mathematical approach — a square or a circle in art are nothing in themselves and are alive only in the instinctive and inspirational use an artist can make of them in expressing a poetic
idea.

— Ben Nicholson

Geometry as foundation

Know oh brother . . . that the study of sensible geometry leads
to skill in all the practical arts, while the study of intelligible
geometry leads to skill in the intellectual arts because this science is one of the gates through which we move to the knowledge of the essence of the soul, and that is the root of all
knowledge.

— From the Rasa 'il by the Brotherhood of Purity

Geometric treasures

Geometry has two great treasures: one is the theorem of Pythagoras; the other, the division of a line into extreme and mean ratio. The first we may compare to a measure of gold; the second we may name a precious jewel.

— Johannes Kepler

The spirit of geometry

Geometry is the Formal structure
    of thought.
The spirit of geometry is the
    structure of Light.
The soul of geometry is the structure of Space.
The structure of Space is
    PURE FORM.

— Irene Rice Pereira

Golden Mean and unity

In a sense, the Golden Proportion can be considered as supra-rational or transcendent. It is actually the first issue of Oneness, the only possible creative duality within Unity. It is the most intimate relationship, one might say, that proportional existence — the universe — can have with Unity, the primal or first division of One. For this reason the ancients called it "golden," the perfect division. . . .

— Robert Lawlor

MODES

Geometry and reason

From this stage, reason advanced to the province of the eyes. And scanning the earth and the heavens, it realized that nothing pleased it but beauty; and in beauty, design; and in design, dimensions; and in dimensions, number. And it asked itself whether any line or curve or any other form or shape in that realm was of such kind as intelligence comprehended. It found that they were far inferior; and that nothing which the eyes beheld could in any way be compared with what the mind discerned. These distinct and separate realities, it also reduced to a branch of learning, and called it geometry.

— Augustine

Geometry as a bridge

Geometry enables its votary, like a bridge, to pass over the obscurity of material nature, as over some dark sea to the luminous regions of perfect reality.

—Thomas Taylor

Mannerism versus spirit

We read the complaints of great men in every century about the customs of their age. They always sound as if they referred to our own age, for the race is always the same. At every time and in every art, mannerisms have taken the place of the spirit, which was always the possession of a few individuals, but mannerisms are just the old cast-off garments of the last manifestation of the spirit that existed and was recognized.

— Arthur Schopenhauer

Ideas in things

No doubt, it is useful for an artist to know all the forms of art which have preceded or which accompany his. That is a sign of strength if it is a question of looking for a stimulus or recognizing mistakes he must avoid. But he must be very careful not to look for models. As soon as an artist takes another as model he is lost. There is no other point of departure than reality. Why should I copy this owl, this sea-urchin? Why should I try to imitate nature? I might just as well try to trace a perfect circle. What I have to do is to utilize as best I can the ideas which objects suggest to me, connect, fuse, and color in my way the shadows they cast within me, illumine them from the inside.

— Pablo Picasso

Beautiful in kind

A recognition of the fact that things can only be beautiful in kind, and not in one another's kinds, and the conception of the formality of beauty, bring us back again to the futility of a naturalistic art; the beauties of a living man and of a statue or stone man are different in kind and not interchangeable; the more we try to make the statue look like a man, the more we denature the stone and caricature the man. It is the form of a man in a nature of flesh that constitutes the beauty of this man; the form of a man in a nature of stone, the beauty of the statue; and these two beauties are incompatible.

— Ananda K. Coomaraswamy

MEANS

Use simple means

Our *search for architecture* has led to the discovery of simplicity. Great art — we must never tire of repeating this — is produced by simple means. History shows that the mind tends toward simplicity. Simplicity, which results from judgments and choices, is a sign of mastery. It gives, through a clearly perceptible play of forms, the means of expressing a state of mind, of revealing a spiritual system. It is like an *affirmation*, a path leading from confusion to clear geometric statements.

. . . *So, simplicity is not equivalent to poverty*; it is a choice, a discrimination, a crystallization. Its object is purity. Simplicity synthesizes. A ragged agglomeration of cubes is an accidental event, but a synthesis is an intellectual act.

— Le Corbusier

Experience of the object

To achieve the conviction and substantiality of things, a reality intensified and potentiated to the point of indestructibility by his experience of the object, this seemed to [Cézanne] to be the purpose of his innermost work.

— Rainer Maria Rilke

Balance of elements

Content without method ends in sentimental chaos; method without content in sophistry: material without form is a deadweight of fact; form without material a spinning of cobwebs.

— Johann Wolfgang von Goethe

150

Monsters, gods, and the human figure

Without monsters and gods, art cannot enact our drama: art's most profound moments express this frustration. When they were abandoned as untenable superstitions, art sank into melancholy. It became fond of the dark, and enveloped its objects in the nostalgic intimations of a half-lit world. For me the great achievements of the centuries in which the artist accepted the probable and familiar as his subjects were the pictures of the single human figure — alone in a moment of utter immobility.

— Mark Rothko

Your own language

Know what the old masters did. Know how they composed their pictures, but do not fall into the conventions they established. These conventions were right for them, and they are wonderful. They made their language. You make yours. They can help you. All the past can help you.

— Robert Henri

The beauty of tools

I love the tools made for mechanics. I stop at windows of hardware stores. If I could only find an excuse to buy many more of them than I have already bought on the mere pretense that I might have use for them! They are so beautiful, so simple and plain and straight to their meaning. There is no "Art" about them, they have not been *made* beautiful, they *are* beautiful.

— Robert Henri

151

ARTICULATION

Form as source

Form is a parenthetical aspect of state. It is evidence of state.

Form is universally consistent in its emotional evocation.

Form evokes feeling.
Feeling conjures metaphor.
Metaphor spawns idea.
Idea demands expression.

> — Gilah Yelin Hirsch

Pure color

Color exists in itself, possesses its own beauty. . . .

Pure colors . . . have in themselves, independently of the objects they serve to express, a significant action on the feelings of those who look at them.

> — Henri Matisse

The reflective object

A real painter never imitates. He uses an object as a recipient of focus of the sun, or to observe a color reflex in that object's surroundings, or to catch, above it, an interweaving of light and darkness. In other words, the thing painted is merely an inducement.

> — Rudolf Steiner

The nature of light

Reduction! One wants to say more than nature and one makes the impossible mistake of wanting to say it with more means than she, instead of fewer. Light and the rational forms are locked in combat; light sets them into motion, bends what is straight, makes parallels oval, inscribes circles in the intervals, makes the intervals active. Hence the inexhaustible variety.

— Paul Klee

Of color alone

The freedom of abstract thought has come, and shows us a future lying ahead of color as one of the three great abstract arts.

Mathematics — music — color. To those artists whose inspiration comes in the form of shape and shape relationships, color may continue to be the means of expressing those shapes, unless it be that they find that light and shade is a more suitable means for their purpose.

But to those artists whose inspiration comes in the form of color, of color alone, without reference to object or object sense, it is no longer necessary to set about seeking some form into which the color may be tagged to give it being. Naturally color must have area, space — but let that area be directed by the needs of the color itself and not by some consideration of form.

— Winifred Nicholson

ARTICULATION

Unity of color and form

. . . It should be as impossible to separate form from color or color from form as it is to separate wood from wood-color or stone-color from stone. Color exists not as applied paint but as the inner core of an idea and this idea cannot be touched physically any more than one can touch the blue of a summer sky.

— Ben Nicholson

Emotion and color

We can never hope to duplicate Nature anyway — therefore it is better to express one's own feelings. How could one possibly paint real grief — tears that well up from the depths of a person's soul. . . ?

That anguish-racked face had to be painted the way I saw it then against the green walls of the hospital. And the inquiring, suffering eyes of the child I had to paint just as I saw them staring out of the tiny, pallid yellow body as white as the white sheet on which it lay. I had to ignore a lot of other things such as the effect of truth to light, which is relative. Large areas of the picture were like a poster — wide expanses of nothingness. But I hoped to make the best parts, the ones meant to convey the picture's true message of pain, something even more sublime.

— Edvard Munch

ARTICULATION

Experience and color

The large White Flower with the golden heart is something I have to say about White — quite different from what White has been meaning to me. Whether the flower or the color is the focus I do not know. I do know that the flower is painted large to convey to you my experience of the flower — and what is my experience of the flower — if it is not color.

— Georgia O'Keeffe

Absolutely miraculous green

The real revelation came on a visit to Paris about the end of 1920. . . . I remember suddenly coming on a cubist Picasso at the end of a small upstairs room . . . it must have been a 1915 painting — it was what seemed to me then completely abstract and in the center there was an absolutely miraculous green very deep, very potent and absolutely real. . . . It was this painting in among all the other exciting paintings I saw in Paris 1921-22-23 that were such an inspiration. . . .

— Ben Nicholson

PART IX

The Dynamics of
Creative Work

I enter my studio. Work in progress is hanging on the wall — a hapless victim, abandoned in despair, the enthusiasm that fueled it exhausted, the original idea muddled over, no longer evident. I stare — what is it? what does it want to become? An energy is felt — I follow the impulse: I want to do, solve the problem, to save the thing. This misguided onslaught is full of willing and I destroy the thing. I am defeated and give in: I know I have to come to my still point where all potential lies.

The mind at peace, the memory reveals again the thought that wants expression. A new freedom is apparent, the habitual gives way to trust. My consciousness awakened to the task, I become a willing instrument — I enter the stream of power. My attention rests at the tip of the brush — the point of interaction — the field of all potentiality. I am joyful, playful, unencumbered by the past, the how-to. Nothing else matters: no goal, no purpose, no time, no place.

Beginning

Welcome, O life! I go to encounter for the millionth time the reality of experience and to forge in the smithy of my soul the uncreated conscience of my race.

— James Joyce

The invocation

How is the form of the thing to be made evoked? This is the kernel of our doctrine, and the answer can be made in a great many different ways. The art of God is the Son "through whom all things are made"; in the same way the art in the human artist is his child through which some one thing is to be made. The intuition–expression of an imitable form is an intellectual conception born of the artist's wisdom, just as the eternal reasons are born of the Eternal Wisdom. The image arises naturally in his spirit, not by way of an aimless inspiration, but in purposeful and vital operation,[1] "by a word conceived in intellect."[2]

— Ananda K. Coomaraswamy

---

[1]   The conception of an imitable form is a "vital operation," that is to say, a generation.

[2]   St. Thomas Aquinas, Sum. Theol., 1.45.6c

GATHERING FORCES

A marvelous mounting force

Of its very nature, work is a manifold instrument of detachment . . . it implies effort and a victory over inertia . . . is always accompanied by the painful pangs of birth. Men can only escape the terrible boredom of monotonous and commonplace duty to find themselves a prey to the inner tension and anxieties of "creation." To create, or organize, material energy, or truth, or beauty, brings with it an inner torment which prevents those who face its hazards from sinking into the quiet and closed-in life wherein grows the vice of self-regard and attachment (in the technical sense). An honest workman not only surrenders his calm and peace once and for all, but must learn continually to jettison the form which his labor or art or thought first took, and go in search of new forms. To pause, so as to bask in or possess results, would be a betrayal of action. Over and over again he must go beyond himself, tear himself away from himself, leaving behind him his most cherished beginnings. . . . By virtue of a marvelous mounting force contained in things, each reality attained and left behind gives us access to the discovery and pursuit of an ideal of higher spiritual content. . . .

— Teilhard de Chardin

GATHERING FORCES

Inspiration and aspiration

"Through the mouth of Hermes the divine Eros began to speak." We must not conclude from the form of the words that the artist is a passive instrument, like a stenographer. "He" is much rather actively and consciously making use of "himself" as an instrument. Body and mind are not the man, but only his instrument and vehicle. The man is passive only when he identifies himself with the psychophysical ego letting it take him where it will: but in act when he directs it. Inspiration and aspiration are not exclusive alternatives, but one and the same; because the spirit to which both words refer cannot work in the man except to the extent that *he* is "in the spirit."

— Ananda K. Coomaraswamy

A gathering of consciousness

When we approach the Acropolis in Athens, we are conscious of being in the company of all mankind. It is one of the universal places, where the collective mind and soul meet and gather to a point of perception. When Pericles undertook to reconstruct these war-shattered monuments, he knew that the intense, focused vison of thousands of artisans working together would produce a gathering of consciousness on that site which would recapture and preserve the sacred power of a place which had been the source of Athenian strength for a thousand years.

— Richard Geldard

CREATIVE EFFORT

The complete work in mind

When I am, as it were, completely myself, entirely alone, and of good cheer — say, traveling in a carriage, or walking after a good meal, or during the night when I cannot sleep; it is on such occasions that my ideas flow best and most abundantly. Whence and how they come, I know not; nor can I force them. Those ideas that please me I retain in memory, and am accustomed, as I have been told, to hum them to myself. . . . Provided I am not disturbed, my subject enlarges itself, becomes methodized and defined, and the whole, though it be long, stands almost complete and finished in my mind, so that I can survey it, like a fine picture or a beautiful statue, at a glance. Nor do I hear in my imagination the parts successively, but I hear them, as it were, all at once. What a delight this is I cannot tell! All this inventing, this producing, takes place in a pleasing lively dream. . . . The committing to paper is done quickly enough, for everything is, as I said before, already finished; and it rarely differs on paper from what it was in my imagination. . . .

— Wolfgang Amadeus Mozart

Obey the inner command

I advanced consciously to the highest simplicity of expression. . . . The inner command was obeyed still more frequently; to allow oneself to fall into one's own essence.

— Julius Bissier

CREATIVE EFFORT

Genius at work

I carry my thoughts about me for a long time, before I write them down. Meanwhile my memory is so tenacious that I am sure never to forget, not even in years, a theme that has once occurred to me. I change many things, discard and try again until I am satisfied. Then, however, there begins in my head the development in every direction. . . . and there remains for me nothing but the labor of writing it down. . . .

You will ask where my ideas come from. I cannot say for certain. They come uncalled, sometimes independently, sometimes in association with other things. It seems to me that I could wrest them from Nature herself with my own hands, as I go walking in the woods. They come to me in the silence of the night or in the early morning, stirred into being by moods which the poet would translate into words, but which I put into sounds; and these go through my head ringing and singing and storming until at last I have them before me as notes.

— Ludwig von Beethoven

Unseen help

Yes, when I work, when I am submissive and modest, I feel myself so helped by someone who makes me do things that surpass me. Still, I feel no gratitude toward *Him* because it is as if I were faced with a magician whose tricks I can't see through. I feel deprived of the profit of the experience that should have compensated my effort. I am ungrateful without remorse.

— Henri Matisse

CREATIVE EFFORT

The gentle vibration of things

I must learn how to express the gentle vibration of things, their roughened textures, their intricacies . . . the strange quality of expectation that hovers over muted things; I must try to get hold of the great and simple beauty of all that. In general, I must strive for the utmost simplicity united with the most intimate power of observation. That's where greatness lies.

The intensity with which a subject is grasped (still lifes, portraits, or creations of the imagination) — that is what makes for beauty in art.

— Paula Modersohn-Becker

Loyalty in the expression

The manual operation of the artist is called servile, because similitude is with respect to the form; in writing down, for example, the form of a musical composition that has already been heard mentally, or even in performance as such, the artist is no longer free, but an imitator of what he has himself imagined. In such a servility there is certainly nothing dishonorable, but rather a continued loyalty to the good of the work to be done; the artist turns from intellectual to manual operation or vice versa at will, and when the work has been done, he judges its "truth" by measuring the actual form of the artifact against the mental image of it that was his before the work began and remains in his consciousness regardless of what may happen to the work itself.

— Ananda K. Coomaraswamy

CREATIVE EFFORT

Gather and pass on from the depth

May I use a simile, the simile of the tree? The artist has studied this world of variety and has, we may suppose, unobtrusively found his way in it. His sense of direction has brought order into the passing stream of image and experience. This sense of direction in nature and life, this branching and spreading array, I shall compare with the root of the tree.

From the root the sap flows to the artist, flows through him, flows to his eye.

Thus he stands as the trunk of the tree.

Battered and stirred by the strength of the flow, he molds his vision into his work.

As, in full view of the world, the crown of the tree unfolds and spreads in time and in space, so with his work.

Nobody would affirm that the tree grows its crown in the image of its root. Between above and below can be no mirrored reflection. It is obvious that different functions expanding in different elements must produce vital divergences.

But it is just the artist who at times is denied those departures from nature which his art demands. He has even been charged with incompetence and deliberate distortion.

And yet, standing at his appointed place, the trunk of the tree, he does nothing other than gather and pass on what comes to him from the depths. He neither serves nor rules — he transmits.

His position is humble. And the beauty at the crown is not his own. He is merely a channel.

— Paul Klee

CREATIVE EFFORT

Let the hand run free

What matters the most to me? To work with my model until I have it enough in me to be able to improvise, to let my hand run free while respecting the grandeur and sacredness of all living things.

— Henri Matisse

The artist awakens to the task

The artist knows, up to a point, what he or she wishes to express but also feels it, senses it — feels and senses it so strongly that something like awakening has occurred. The ordinary self that entered the studio is still there, but someone else is there as well.

. . . The theme, the task at hand, is clear and unclear. The mind may conceive it precisely or, on the contrary, feelings and the body in motion may have a sense of direction that the mind hardly knows. The forces must come together to serve the theme: the sheer energy and closeness to materials dwelling in the body, the sensitivity to small differences dwelling in the feelings, the organizational clarity and critical capacity of the thought.

. . . Entering more deeply into the creative process, the artist begins to receive spontaneous gifts: signs and meanings suggest themselves "from nowhere" — forms previously unimagined, new themes or motifs that seem remarkably fertile. The working faculties and the companion self have come to life, shedding seeds with abandon and generosity. . . . A degree of spontaneous ability has made itself known, always a gift however much one reaches for it.

— Roger Lipsey

CREATIVE EFFORT

Phases of work

In all the creative work that I have done, what has come first is a problem, a puzzle involving discomfort. Then comes a concentrated voluntary application involving great effort. After this, a period without conscious thought, and finally a solution bringing with it the complete plan of a book. . . .

— Bertrand Russell

Seeking new expression

In my productive activity, every time a type grows beyond the stage of its genesis, and I have about reached the goal, the intensity gets lost very quickly, and I have to look for new ways. It is precisely the way which is productive — this is the essential thing; becoming is more important than being. . . .

— Paul Klee

Attuned to the material

While carving stone, you discover the spirit of your material and the properties peculiar to it. Your hand thinks and follows the thought of the material.

— Constantin Brancusi

Coming full circle

I have a number of ways of working, and they are all part of the same way, and I seldom discard ways, but add to them and use the old ones and carry them all with me as I do my life from childhood. I want to express my feelings and thoughts, and I want to distill them so they will be pristine and clear and come back at me . . . with a new life they never had when inside me.

— Dorothy Dehner

Living the creation again

The discoveries of science, the works of art are explorations — more, are explosions, of a hidden likeness. The discoverer or the artist presents in them two aspects of nature and fuses them into one. This is the act of creation in which an original thought is born, and it is the same act in original science and original art. . . . [This view] alone gives a meaning to the act of appreciation; for the appreciator must see the movement, wake to the echo which was started in the creation of the work. In the moment of appreciation we live again the moment when the creator saw and held the hidden likeness. . . . We re-enact the creative act, and we ourselves make the discovery again. . . . The great poem and the deep theorem are new to every reader, and yet are his own experiences, because he himself re-creates them. They are the marks of unity in variety, and in the instant when the mind seizes this for itself, the heart misses a beat.

— J. Bronowski

Begin in stillness

Each day of rehearsal for a new ballet I arrive at a little before two in the afternoon, and sit alone in my studio to have a moment of stillness before the dancers enter. I tease myself and say I am cultivating my Buddha nature; but it is really just such a comforting place for me to be — secure, clear, and with a purpose. . . . I sit with my back to our large mirrors so that I am completely within myself.

— Martha Graham

Expressive silences

When I first visited Mondrian's studio it was his silences and the feeling of his thought in the studio which moved me. I am not interested to read what he wrote because I get all I need from the feeling of his original thought and from those most expressive silences in certain periods of his painting.

— Ben Nicholson

Order in the workplace

If anyone wishes to see how the soul dwells in its body, let him observe how this body uses its daily habitation; that is to say, if this is devoid of order and confused, the body will be kept in disorder and confusion by its soul. . . .

— Leonardo da Vinci

Joy in the work

Will power, the kind that, if need be, makes us set our teeth and endure suffering, is the principal weapon of the apprentice engaged in manual work. But, contrary to the usual belief, it has practically no place in study. The intelligence can only be led by desire. For there to be desire, there must be pleasure and joy in the work. The intelligence only grows and bears fruit in joy. The joy of learning is as indispensable in study as breathing is in running. Where it is lacking there are no real students, but only poor caricatures of apprentices who, at the end of their apprenticeship, will not even have a trade.

— Simone Weil

Revelation in the work

I am simply conscious of the forces I am using and I am driven on by an idea that I really only grasp as it grows with the picture.

— Henri Matisse

Marriage of opposites

Some collaboration has to take place in the mind between the woman and the man before the art of creation can be accomplished. Some marriage of opposites has to be consummated. The whole of the mind must lie wide open if we are to get the sense that the writer is communicating his experience with perfect fullness.

— Virginia Woolf

STATES OF MIND

Seizing the intuitive moment

Ideally a painter (and, generally, an artist) should not become conscious of his insights: without taking the detour through his reflective processes, and incomprehensibly to himself, all his progress should enter so swiftly into the work that he is unable to recognize them in the moment of transition. Alas, the artist who waits in ambush there, watching, detaining them, will find them transformed like the beautiful gold in the fairy tale which cannot remain gold because some small detail was not taken care of.

— Rainer Maria Rilke

On its own wings

The supply comes to us artists from the source of all of everything, as you know, whenever an idea comes of itself on its own wings. That is an inexhaustible source and the same impetus which sends the idea brings with it the power of carrying it out, which implies nourishment, shelter, friends, peace of mind, everything. The only thing one has to do is not block up the channels through which the supply comes, and not to think, "I must make some money. My genius must support me. I must." That is like going up into the high heavens to bring down a special pocketful of sunlight for oneself.

— Winifred Nicholson

Not conscious of myself

I have a lover's clear sight or a lover's blindness. . . . I shall do another picture this very night, and I shall bring it off. I have a terrible lucidity at moments when nature is so beautiful; I am not conscious of myself any more, and the picture comes to me as in a dream. . . .

— Vincent van Gogh

Recollection, not excitement

Good art is no more a matter of moods than good conduct a matter of inclination; both are habits; it is the recollected man, and not the excited man, who can either make or do well.

— Ananda K. Coomaraswamy

Approaching prayer

For me, [this project] is essentially a work of art. I meditate, and let myself be penetrated by what I'm undertaking. I do not know if I have faith or not. Perhaps I'm somewhat Buddhist. The essential thing is to work in a state of mind that approaches prayer.

My only religion is that of love for the work to be created, love of creation and of great sincerity. . . .

— Henri Matisse

STATES OF MIND

Everything has me

I don't want anything in the world — I just like existing every minute, and watching things coming and things going, and then coming again, like storms and sunshine and then storms again. I don't want anything at all for the simple reason that I have everything, or rather, which is the same thing, everything has me. . . .

— Winifred Nicholson

Objectivity

How great this watching of [Cézanne] was and how unimpeachably accurate, is almost touchingly confirmed by the fact that, without even remotely interpreting his expression or presuming himself superior to it, he reproduced himself with so much humble objectivity, with the unquestioning, matter-of-fact interest of a dog who sees himself in a mirror and thinks: there's another dog.

— Rainer Maria Rilke

Approaching the spontaneous

The performance of the acrobat appears easy and relaxed, but let us not lose sight of the long preliminary ordeal which enables him to give this effect. It is the same in painting. With hard work, the mastery of one's medium should pass from the conscious to the subconscious; only then can one successfully give an impression of spontaneity. . . .

— Henri Matisse

STATES OF MIND

The present moment

This moment of rehearsal is the instant I care about. This is the very now of my life.

The only thing we have is the now. You begin from the now, what you know, and move into the old, ancient ones that you did not know but which you find as you go along. I think you only find the past from yourself, from what you are experiencing now, what enters your life at the present moment.

— Martha Graham

Seizing the moment

One must be so deeply absorbed in it that within a short time something is created on the paper or the canvas, where at first there was nothing, so that later one hardly knows oneself how one hammered it off. The time for reasoning and deliberating must go before the resolute action. During the doing itself there is little room for deliberating and reasoning.

— Vincent van Gogh

The state of being in the stroke

It is not enough to have thought great things *before* doing the work. The brush stroke at the moment of contact carries inevitably the exact state of being of the artist at that exact moment into the work. . . .

— Robert Henri

STATES OF MIND

Serve the moment

Right now a moment of time is fleeting by! Capture its reality in paint! To do that we must put all else out of our minds. We must become that moment, make ourselves a sensitive recording plate . . . give the image of what we actually see, forgetting everything that has been seen before our time.

Surely, a single bunch of carrots painted naively just as we personally see it is worth all the endless banalities of the Schools, all those dreary pictures concocted out of tobacco juice according to time-honored formulas? The day is coming when a single carrot, freshly observed, will set off a revolution.

— Paul Cézanne

Crazy with joy

Here I am . . . happy, completely happy. I have had a wonderful day of painting. It is not that I have accomplished anything in particular, but it's the thought of all I could do that makes me almost crazy with joy.

— Paula Modersohn-Becker

The means, not the end

And as to art, to say that the artist works for art is an abuse of language. Art is that *by* which a man works, supposing that he is in possession of his art and has the habit of his art; just as prudence or conscience is that by which he acts well. Art is no more the end of his work than prudence the end of his conduct.

— Ananda K. Coomaraswamy

BEYOND DOING

Working without doing

The softest thing in the universe
Overcomes the hardest thing in the universe.
That without substance can enter where there is no room.
Hence I know the value of non-action.

Teaching without words and work without doing
Are understood by very few.

— Lao Tsu

Creating, yet not possessing

Therefore the sage goes about doing nothing, teaching
no-talking.
The ten thousand things rise and fall without cease,
Creating, yet not possessing,
Working, yet not taking credit.
Work is done, then forgotten.
Therefore it lasts forever.

— Lao Tsu

Detachment

The artist must work with indifferency. Too great interest viti-
ates his work.

— Henry David Thoreau

175

Willingly but not by will

The artist has some "inkling" of God's manner of working "willingly but not by will, naturally and not by nature" when he has acquired mastery and the habit of his work and does not hesitate but can go ahead without a qualm, not wondering, am I right or am I doing wrong? If the painter had to plan out every brush mark before he made his first he would not paint at all.

— Ananda K. Coomaraswamy

Renunciation

The balance between warm susceptibility to impressions and cool judgment, between which the artist continually swings to and fro, can only be found in self-conquest and subsequent self-control. The happiest and proudest artist will be he who most easily achieves renunciation. I mean renunciation in the highest sense of the word — that which lies in not exhibiting one's talent and knowledge, and using them only in so far as they are relevant. Because it will prove to be a fact that a mere excess of artistic power will not make the solution of even the simplest artistic problem easy; for a perfect solution even the most extraordinary powers will hardly suffice. . . .

The artist must lift himself above all external circumstances, even above himself. For, last but not least, he must in his works achieve a bold and unhampered resolution that denies all pain and trouble. . . .

— Hans Von Marées

Mindfulness

A painter seats himself before his pupils. He examines his brush and slowly makes it ready for use, carefully rubs ink, straightens the long strip of paper that lies before him on the mat, and finally, after lapsing for a while into profound concentration, in which he sits like one inviolable, he produces with rapid, absolutely sure strokes a picture which, capable of no further correction and needing none, serves the class as a model.

[The Masters] carry out the preliminary movements musingly and composedly, they efface themselves in the process of shaping and creating, and to both the pupils and themselves it seems like a self-contained event from the first opening maneuvers to the completed work. And indeed the whole thing has such expressive power that it affects the beholder like a picture.

The meditative repose in which he performs [the preparations] gives him that vital loosening and equability of all his powers, that collectedness and presence of mind, without which no right work can be done. Sunk without purpose in what he is doing, he is brought face to face with that moment when the work, hovering before him in ideal line, realizes itself as if of its own accord.

— Eugen Herrigel

ATTENTION

Mind and will alert

No work may be begun so well or done so skillfully that one may feel free and secure in his progress and then let mind relax or go to sleep. One should always go at his work with the twin agents, mind and will, alert; and thus he will do his best in the highest sense of the word and guard intelligently against apparent and subtle faults. Thus he will avoid mistakes, and progress without faltering to greater things.

— Meister Eckhart

The nature of attention

We should also understand the qualitative difference between concentration and attention. . . . To concentrate implies bringing all your energy to focus on a certain point; but thought wanders away and so you have a perpetual battle between the desire to concentrate, to give all your energy to look at a page, and the mind which is wandering, and which you try to control. Whereas attention has no control, no concentration. It is complete attention, which means giving all your energy, your nerves, the capacity, the energy of the brain, your heart, everything, to attending. . . . When you do attend so completely there is no recording and no action from memory.

— J. Krishnamurti

Unity of hand and mind

. . . Mastery in ink-painting is only attained when the hand, exercising perfect control over technique, executes what hovers before the mind's eye at the same moment when the mind begins to form it, without there being a hair's breadth between. Painting then becomes spontaneous calligraphy. . . .

— Eugen Herrigel

Unity of expression

. . . The right frame of mind for the artist is only reached when the preparing and the creating, the technical and the artistic, the material and the spiritual, the project and the object, flow together without a break. . . .

— Eugen Herrigel

Contemplation in the work

The man incapable of contemplation cannot be an artist, but only a skillful workman; it is demanded of the artist to be both a contemplative and a good workman. Best of all if, like the angels, he need not in his activity "lose the delights of inward contemplation."

— Ananda K. Coomaraswamy

Endless leisure

Great works of art have endless leisure for a background, as universe has space. Time stands still while they are created. The artist cannot be in a hurry. The earth moves round the sun with inconceivable rapidity, and yet the surface of the lake is not ruffled by it. . . .

— Henry David Thoreau

Proceeding slowly

I proceed very slowly, nature offering itself to me with great complexity, and the need for progress incessant. One has to see the model and sense very rightly; and beyond that to express oneself with distinctiveness and force.

— Paul Cézanne

Taking time

Sometimes I dream of a work of really great breadth, ranging through the whole region of element, object, meaning, and style.

This, I fear, will remain a dream, but it is a good thing even now to bear the possibility occasionally in mind.

Nothing can be rushed. It must grow, it should grow of itself, and if the time ever comes for that work — then so much the better!

— Paul Klee

MEASURE

Moderation

Therefore the sage is sharp but not cutting,
Pointed but not piercing,
Straightforward but not unrestrained.,
Brilliant but not blinding.

— Lao Tsu

Fine tuning

The artist must attune himself to that which wants to reveal itself
and permit the process to happen through him.

— Martin Heidegger

Taste and moderation

Be not too tame neither, but let your own discretion be your
tutor. Suit the action to the word, the word to the action; with
this special observance, that you o'erstep not the modesty of
nature; for anything so o'erdone is from the purpose of playing,
whose end, both at the first and now, was and is to hold, as
'twere, the mirror up to nature; to show virtue her own feature,
scorn her own image, and the very age and body of the time his
form and pressure.

— **William Shakespeare,** *Hamlet*

METHOD

No plan, no greatness

The plan is basic. Where there is no plan, there is no greatness of intention and expression, no rhythm, no volume, no coherence. Where there is no plan, we experience that sensation of formlessness, indigence, disorder, unreason, that the human mind cannot endure.

The plan calls for a highly active imagination. It also calls for severe self-discipline. The plan determines everything else; it is the decisive moment.

— Le Corbusier

Rousing ourselves from sleep

Whenever I find myself growing vaporish, I rouse myself, wash and put on a clean shirt, brush my hair and clothes, tie my shoestrings neatly, and in fact adonize as I were going out — then, all clean and comfortable, I sit down to write.

— John Keats

Simple gazing

The first thing I do when I am conscious of the coming of a poem is to seek paper and pencil. It seems as though the simple gazing at a piece of blank paper hypnotizes me into an awareness of the subconscious. . . . I find that the concentration needed for this is in the nature of a trance. . . .

— Amy Lowell

Point of departure

I work in a state of passion and compulsion. When I begin a canvas, I obey a physical impulse, a need to act; it's like a physical discharge. . . . I begin my pictures under the effect of a shock. . . . which makes me escape from reality. The cause of this shock may be a tiny thread sticking out of the canvas, a drop of water falling, this print made by my finger on the shining surface of this table. . . . I need a point of departure, even if it's only a speck of dust or a flash of light. This form begets a series of things, one thing giving birth to another thing.

— Joan Miró

Arousing the imagination

I cannot forbear to mention among these precepts a new device for study which although it may seem but trivial and almost ludicrous, is nevertheless extremely useful in arousing the mind to various inventions. And this is, when you look at a wall spotted with stains, or with a mixture of stones, if you have to devise some scene, you may discover a resemblance to various landscapes, beautified with mountains, rivers, rocks, trees, plains, wide valleys, and hills in varied arrangement; or again you may see battles and figures in action; or strange faces and costumes, and an endless variety of objects, which you could reduce to complete and well drawn forms. And these appear on such walls confusedly, like the sound of bells in whose jangle you may find any name or word you choose to imagine.

— Leonardo da Vinci

183

METHOD

Letting the lava cool

Do not finish your work too much. An impression is not sufficiently durable for its first freshness to survive a belated search for infinite detail; in this way you let the lava grow cool and turn boiling blood into a stone. . . .

— Paul Gauguin

Finding the point of re-entry

My reaction at each stage is as important as the subject. . . . It is a continuous process until the moment when my work is in harmony with me. At each stage I reach a balance, a conclusion. The next time I return to the work, if I discover a weakness in the unity, I find my way back into the picture by means of the weakness — I return through the breach — and I conceive the whole afresh. Thus the whole thing comes alive again.

— Henri Matisse

The materials and touch

. . . I am afloat, I sail on the infinite combinations of the materials I touch. I believe that the artist yields often to the stimuli of materials that will transmit his spirit. I am certain about what I will never do; but not about what my art will render. I await joyous surprises while working, an awakening of the materials that I work and that my spirit develops. The good work proceeds with tenacity, intention, without interruption, with an equal measure of passion and reason and it must surpass the goal the artist has set for himself.

— Odilon Redon

METHOD

Begin in nature

. . . I would like architects — not just students — to pick up a pencil and draw a plant, a leaf, the spirit of a tree, the harmony of a sea shell, formations of clouds, the complex play of waves spreading out on a beach, so as to discover different expressions of an inner force. I would like their hands and minds to become passionately involved in this kind of intimate investigation.

— Le Corbusier

To the end

People usually fail when they are on the verge of success.
So give as much care to the end as to the beginning;
Then there will be no failure.

— Lao Tsu

STRUGGLE

Be not satisfied

Assuredly, wherever mind rises above instruments and material, as befits it, the work never satisfies the workman. In truth that man never satisfies art whom artistry always satisfies.

— Marsilio Ficino

Not afraid of it

I have been depressed for days. Profoundly sad and solemn. I think the time is coming for struggle and uncertainty. It comes into every serious and beautiful life. I knew all along that it had to come. I've been expecting it. I am not afraid of it. I know it will mature and help me develop.

— Paula Modersohn-Becker

Redeem the time

Where art thou, Muse, that thou forget'st so long
To speak of that which gives thee all thy might?
Spend'st thou thy fury on some worthless song,
Dark'ning thy power to lend base subjects light?
Return, forgetful Muse, and straight redeem
In gentle numbers time so idly spent;
Sing to the ear that doth thy lays esteem
And gives thy pen both skill and argument. . . .

— William Shakespeare

The mystery of the process

In a certain way I am glad I have not *learned* painting. . . .

I *do not know myself* how I paint it. I sit down with a white board before the spot that strikes me, I look at what is before my eyes, and say to myself, that white board must become something; I come back dissatisfied — I put it away, and when I have rested a little, I go and look at it with a kind of fear. Then I am still dissatisfied, because I still have that splendid scene too clearly in my mind to be satisfied with what I have made of it. But I find in my work an echo of what struck me. . . .

— Vincent van Gogh

Clarify the original image

Half-way through any work, one is often tempted to go off on a tangent. But then one knows that there can be no end to such temptations, such abandonments of one's plan. Once you have yielded, you will be tempted to yield again and again as you progress on a single job. Finally, you would only produce something hybrid, so I always resist these temptations and try to impose my will on the material, allowing myself only, as I work, to clarify the original image. At the same time, one must be entirely sensitive to the structure of the material that one is handling. One must yield to it in tiny details of execution, perhaps the handling of the surface or grain, and one must master it as a whole.

— Barbara Hepworth

STRUGGLE

Resolving conflict

I learned to battle with the canvas, to come to know it as a being resisting my wish, and to bend it forcibly to this wish. At first it stands there like a pure chaste virgin with clear eye and heavenly joy — this pure canvas which itself is as *beautiful* as a painting. And then comes the willful brush which first here, then there, gradually conquers it with all the energy peculiar to it, like a European colonist who pushes into the wild virgin nature, hitherto untouched, using axe, spade, hammer, and saw to shape it to his wishes. I have gradually learned not to see the resistant white of the canvas, to notice it only for instants (as a control), instead of seeing in it the tones that are to replace it — thus one thing slowly followed another.

— Wassily Kandinsky

No matter what

I have painted every day and more and more to my satisfaction, so no matter if hunks of my flesh fall off my feet where I froze them standing on this cold floor.

— Dorothy Dehner

Image, will, and the material

[My works are] an imitation of my own past and present and of my own creative vitality as I experience them in one particular instant of my emotional and imaginative life. . . .

I must always have a clear image of the form of a work before I begin. Otherwise there is no impulse to create. The kind of sculpture that I indulge in is hard work, and I would always hesitate to start doodling with a mass of wood or stone as if I were waiting for the form to develop out of the work. Still, the preconceived form is always connected with a material. I think of it as stone, or as bronze, or as wood, and I then carry out the project accordingly, imposing my own will on the material. The size of the sculpture is also important, in my first clear image of what I want to do. I can see the material that I want to work on, and also the exact relationship of the object to its surroundings, I mean its scale.

— Barbara Hepworth

On the dark path

A foggy day. Spending the day on the dark path, feeling out my own resistance. The yearning to be connected, and my unwillingness to reach out. The terrible wish to create, and my reluctance to do it. Feeling, observing, agonizing.

— Burghild Nina Holzer

STRUGGLE

Out of the darkness

The organic laws of construction tangled me in my desires, and only with great pain, effort, and struggle did I break through these "walls around art." Thus did I finally enter the realm of art, which like that of nature, science, political forms, etc., is a realm unto itself, is governed by its own laws proper to it alone, and which together with the other realms ultimately forms the great realm which we can only dimly divine.

Today is the great day of one of the revelations of this world. The interrelationships of these individual realms were illumined as by a flash of lightning; they burst unexpected, frightening, and joyous out of the darkness. Never were they so strongly tied together and never so sharply divided. This lightning is the child of the darkening of the spiritual heaven which hung over us, black, suffocating, and dead. Here begins the epoch of the spiritual, the revelation of the spirit. . . .

— Wassily Kandinsky

Complexities of purpose

Unconscious insights or answers to problems that come in reverie do not come hit or miss. They may indeed occur at times of relaxation, or in fantasy, or at other times when we alternate play with work. But what is entirely clear is that they pertain to those areas in which the person consciously has worked laboriously and with dedication. *Purpose* in the human being is a much more complex phenomenon than what used to be called will power. Purpose involves all levels of experience. We cannot *will* to have insights. We cannot *will* creativity. But we can *will* to give ourselves to the encounter with intensity of dedication and commitment. The deeper aspects of awareness are activated to the extent that the person is committed to the encounter.

— Rollo May

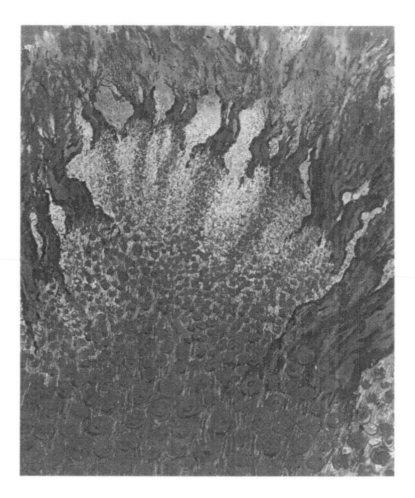

PART X

The Experience of the Creative Life

There is a duality in my life; I need to go within, work in solitude, work until I'm spent without regard to demands from without, to shun the marketplace; and yet, I need to interact with the world, to walk in the woods, to exchange ideas. There is the need to exhibit, the desire for some critical acclaim; I need feedback to justify my existence. Yet, success and failure in the marketplace have to be met with detachment. What really matters is what takes place in the moment of creation. The reward, the inner satisfaction, is in the work.

Every now and then I need to recreate myself. The signal is a sense of boredom with what I'm doing. I need to stop producing, re-think my role, question my motives, replenish the well. At times this is an active inquiry in the mind; at other times, I quench my thirst with the great sacred texts, and yet another time, I meditate and reflect and, by grace, experience new dimensions.

Self-discovery and the search for truth and beauty through creativity are essentially the same. There is always more to be seen and more to be communicated. I have learned to wait for these insights and not to despair when the light is hidden; it will reveal itself again anew.

193

The laws of the creative life

Movement never lies. It is a barometer telling the state of the soul's weather to all who can read it. This might be called the law of the dancer's life — the law which governs its outer aspects.

Then comes cultivation of the being from which whatever you have to say comes. It doesn't just come out of nowhere, it comes out of a great curiosity. . . . There is only one of you in the world, just one, and if that is not fulfilled then something has been lost. Ambition is not enough; necessity is everything. It is through this that the legends of the soul's journey are retold with all their tragedy and their bitterness and sweetness of living. It is at this point that the sweep of life catches up with the mere personality of the performer, and while the individual becomes greater, the personal becomes less personal. And there is grace. I mean the grace resulting from faith . . . faith in life, in love, in people, in the act of dancing. All this is necessary to any performance in life which is magnetic, powerful, rich in meaning.

— Martha Graham

No shortage of work

All is "well" with me. The rain doesn't reach me, my room is well heated, what more can one ask for? There's no shortage of work, either — on the contrary. . . .

— Paul Klee

Unity and genuineness

Surely all art is the result of one's having been in danger, of having gone through an experience all the way to the end, to where no one can go any further. The further one goes, the more private, the more personal, the more singular an experience becomes, and the thing one is making is, finally, the necessary, irrepressible, and, as nearly as possible, definitive utterance of this singularity. . . . Therein lies the enormous aid the work of art brings to the life of the one who must make it, — that it is his epitome; the knot in the rosary at which his life recites a prayer, the ever-returning proof to himself of his unity and genuineness, which presents itself only to him while appearing anonymous to the outside, nameless, existing merely as necessity, as reality, as being . . . .

— Rainer Maria Rilke

The art and life we deserve

Unfortunately, we do not desire to be such as the Shaker was; we do not propose to "work as though we had a thousand years to live, and as though we were to die tomorrow." Just as we desire peace but not the things that make for peace, so we desire art but not the things that make for art. We put the cart before the horse. *Il pittore pinge se stesso;* we have the art that we deserve. If the sight of it puts us to shame, it is with ourselves that the re-formation must begin. A drastic transvaluation of accepted values is required. With the re-formation of man, the arts of peace will take care of themselves.

— Ananda K. Coomaraswamy

Getting through to the work

One works because I suppose it is the most interesting thing one knows to do. The days one works are the best days. On the other days one is hurrying through the other things one imagines one has to do to keep one's life going . . . with a certain amount of aggravation so that you can get at the paintings again because that is the high spot — in a way it is what you do all the other things for.

. . . The painting is like a thread that runs through all the reasons for all the other things that make one's life.

—Georgia O'Keeffe

Inspiration in the commonplace

I wish to live ever as to derive my satisfactions and inspirations from the commonest events, every-day phenomena, so that what my senses hourly perceive, my daily walk, the conversation of my neighbors, may inspire me, and I may dream of no heaven but that which lies about me.

— Henry David Thoreau

One long investigation

An artist must educate himself, he cannot be educated, he must test things out as they apply to himself; his life is one long investigation of things and his own reaction to them. If he is to be interesting to us it is because he renders a very personal account.

— Robert Henri

196

Passion, conviction and discovery

Someone remarked that it must take great patience to make my reliefs. This is to misunderstand the whole nature of how an artist works — surely it is only as the result of an *irresistible* inner urge that he works, that he is capable of making a fresh discovery. It is passion not patience which comes into the matter. Patience can be explained, passion cannot. This urge functions with conviction on its first appearance but there must be a discovery as fresh and as vital throughout an artist's life. Very few artists achieve this, and only too often there is no longer any discovery, any reality but only an echo of previous discoveries made by himself. Cézanne is a perfect example of a painter who mastered this problem.

    — Ben Nicholson

The search for faith

Art for art's sake is an empty phrase. Art for the sake of the true, art for the sake of the good and the beautiful, that is the faith I am searching for.

    — George Sand

Living fully

The best art the world has ever had is but the impress left by men who have thought less of making great art than of living fully and completely with all their faculties in the enjoyment of full play. From these the result is inevitable.

    — Robert Henri

DAY-TO-DAY

Eternity in each moment

Take time by the forelock. Now or never. You must live in the present, launch yourself on every wave, find your eternity in each moment. Fools stand on their island opportunities and look toward another land. There is no other land; there is no other life but this, or the like of this.

— Henry David Thoreau

Art, work, and the self

Both art and work, then, should be modes of *making* and *being* and it is man who *is* and *does*. Just as there is no art without some work, so there should be no work without some art. Thus all who are actively involved in work should be in some sense artists just as all artists are workmen, to the extent at least that each seeks to achieve some mastery over his material, to effect its transformation, and to the extent that such transformation properly accomplished will involve mastery over oneself. . . .

— Brian Keeble

A hundred ways to be

Today, like every other day, we wake up empty
and frightened. Don't open the door to the study
and begin reading. Take down the dulcimer.
Let the beauty we love be what we do.
There are hundreds of ways to kneel
and kiss the ground.

— Jalal'uddin Rumi

DAY-TO-DAY

Only time reveals

We know not yet what we have done, still less what we are doing. Wait till evening and other parts of our day's work will shine than we had thought at noon, and we shall discover the real purport of our toil.

In the long run men hit only what they aim at. Therefore, though they should fail immediately, they had better aim at something high.

— Henry David Thoreau

Just climb a few steps

In earlier days (even as a child), the beauty of landscapes was quite clear to me. A background for the soul's moods. Now dangerous moments occur when Nature tries to devour me; at such times I am annihilated, but at peace. This would be fine for old people but I . . . I am my life's debtor, for I have given promises. . . . Frightened, I jump up from the bank, the struggle begins anew. Bitterness has returned. I am not Pan in the reed, I am merely a human being and want to climb a few steps, but really climb them. . . .

— Paul Klee

Conversations

An art student should read, or talk a great deal with those who have read. His conversations with his intimate fellow-students should be more of his life and less of paint.

— Robert Henri

The futility of explanation

Everyone wants to understand art. Why not try to understand the song of a bird? Why does one love the night, flowers, everything around one, without trying to understand them? But in the case of a painting people have to understand. If only they would realize above all that an artist works of necessity, that he himself is only a trifling bit of the world, and that no more importance should be attached to him than to plenty of other things which please us in the world, though we can't explain them. People who try to explain pictures are usually barking up the wrong tree.

— Pablo Picasso

Ignore the trends

The newest trend and the art scene are unnecessary distractions for a serious artist. He will be much more rewarded responding to art of all times and places. Not as art history but considering each piece and its value to him.

— Agnes Martin

Work more, talk less

It is a mistake for a sculptor or a painter to speak or write very often about his job. It releases tension needed for his work. By trying to express his aims with rounded-off logical exactness, he can easily become a theorist whose actual work is only a caged-in exposition of conceptions evolved in terms of logic and words.

— Henry Moore

200

The poetic life

To the poet all things are friendly and sacred, all events profitable, all days holy, all men divine.

— Ralph Waldo Emerson

A trace

Art is, after all, only a trace — like a footprint which shows that one has walked bravely and in great happiness.

Robert Henri

Open to good influences

If one can keep one's mind really open — open to good influences without any attachment to success or failure, without any agitation in the mind, or laziness in handling anything which comes before one in the course of one's daily life, then in spite of all the difficulties, one will keep on improving one's inner being and the world in which one lives. That is the way to live.

—H. H. Shantanand Saraswati

RECOGNITION

No leisure for trifles

Why seek to embarrass [the artist] with vanities foreign to his quietness? Know you not that certain sciences require the whole man, leaving no part of him at leisure for your trifles? . . . You only know this man and praise him in order to do yourselves honor, and are delighted if he be found worthy of the conversation of a pope or an emperor. And I would even venture to affirm that a man cannot attain excellence if he satisfy the ignorant and not those of his own craft, and if he be not "singular" or "distant," or whatever you like to call him.

— Michelangelo

Self-affirmation

Very idle is all curiosity concerning other people's estimate of us, and all fear of remaining unknown is not less so. If a man know that he can do anything, — that he can do it better than anyone else, — he has a pledge of the acknowledgment of that fact by all persons. . . .

— Ralph Waldo Emerson

The company of gods

A real artist may create his picture in a lonely desert. He does not worry about who will look at his picture or whether anybody at all will look at it, for he creates within a divine–spiritual community. Gods look over his shoulder; he creates in their company. What does he care whether or not anybody admires his picture. A person may be an artist in complete loneliness.

— Rudolf Steiner

RECOGNITION

The limits of criticism

Art is there to be seen, not talked about, except perhaps in its presence.

— Johann Wolfgang von Goethe

Purity of early work

Artists who have won fame are embarrassed by it; thus their first works are often their best.

— Ludwig van Beethoven

Be suspicious

. . . One comes back to the thought that every recognition (with very rare, unmistakable exceptions) should make one mistrustful of one's own work. Basically, if it is good, one can't live to see it recognized: otherwise it's just half good and not heedless enough.

— Rainer Maria Rilke

Dangers of success

Success is dangerous. One begins to copy oneself, and to copy oneself is more dangerous than to copy others. It leads to sterility.

— Pablo Picasso

RECOGNITION

Criticism: the noxious cloud

That undisturbed, direct manner of working, almost like a sleep-walker, which alone can lead to greatness, is almost impossible now. All our talents are pilloried in the marketplace. Critical reviews appear every day in fifty different places and the gossip they spread abroad stifles all healthy growth. Whoever does not keep away from it all and insist on isolating himself is lost. True, the criticisms of art and literature in the papers, always bad and usually negative, have brought a kind of half-culture to the masses. But to productive talent this is a noxious cloud dripping poison and destroying the tree of creative life from its green leaves to the core and the very fibers of its roots.

— Johann Wolfgang von Goethe

If the work is true . . .

If your work of art is good, if it is true, it will find its echo and make its place — in six months, in six years, or after you are gone. What is the difference?

— Gustave Flaubert

The eternal in art

Methinks hereafter in some later spring
Echo will bear to men the songs we sing.

— Sappho

RECOGNITION

True criticism

A man of genius or a work of love and beauty will not come to order, can't be compounded by the best rules, but is always a new and incalculable result, like health. Don't rattle your rules in our ears; we must behave as we can. Criticism is an art when it does not stop at the words of the poet, but looks at the order of his thoughts and the essential quality of his mind. Then the critic is poet. 'Tis a question not of talents but of tone; and not particular merits, but the mood of mind into which one and another can bring us.

— Ralph Waldo Emerson

The perfect mind

Do not seek fame. Do not make plans. Do not be absorbed by activities. Do not think that you know. Be aware of all that is and dwell in the infinite. Wander where there is no path. Be all that heaven gave you, but act as though you have received nothing. Be empty, that is all.

— Chuang Tsu

RECOGNITION

The work stands alone

When a painter speaks he speaks badly, but when his painting speaks it speaks well. . . .

Vain is that artist who seeks honor from anyone rather than from the work itself, for the virtue of a work does not depend on him who judges it; rather does the work commend the artist to the judge. . . .

— Marsilio Ficino

Without dwelling

Therefore the sage works without recognition.
He achieves what has to be done without dwelling on it.
He does not try to show his knowledge.

— Lao Tsu

Know your work

If a person withdraws into himself, with all his powers, mental and physical, he comes at last to a condition in which he has no ideas and no limitations and in which he exists without activity of inner or outward life.

He should observe, then, whether or not he is moved to come back to life, but if he finds that he has no urge to get back to work or responsible activity, then he should break loose and get to work of some kind, mental or physical. For a man should never be content [with such indulgence] however good it may be or seem to be, which really does violence to his nature. . . .

Not that one should give up, neglect or forget his inner life for a moment, but he must learn to work in it, with it and out of it, so that the unity of his soul may break out into his activities and his activities shall lead him back to the unity. . . .

— Meister Eckhart

Know which path

When the heavens are obscured to us, and nothing noble or heroic appears, but we are oppressed by imperfection and shortcoming on all hands, we are apt to suck our thumbs and decry our fates. As if nothing was to be done in cloudy weather, or, if heaven were not accessible by the upper road, men would not find a lower. There are two ways to victory — to strive bravely, or to yield. How much pain the last will save us we have not yet learned.

— Henry David Thoreau

A sacred space

A sacred space is any space that is set apart from the usual context of life. . . . Sacred space has no function in the way of earning a living or a reputation. Practical use is not the dominant feature of anything in the space. . . . Your sacred space is where you can find yourself again and again. . . . You really don't have a sacred space, a rescue land, until you find somewhere to be that's not a wasteland, some field of action where there is a spring of ambrosia — a joy that comes from inside, not something external that puts joy into you — a place that lets you experience your own will and your own intention and your own wish so that, in small, the Kingdom is there.

— Joseph Campbell

Close to the infinite

The dimension that counts for the creative person is the space he creates within himself. This inner space is much closer to the infinite than the other, and it is the privilege of a balanced mind — and the search for an equilibrium is essential — to be as aware of inner space as he is of outer space.

— Mark Tobey

Solitude

It seems to me that today, if the artist wishes to be serious to cut out a little original niche for himself, or at least preserve his own innocence of personality — he must once more sink himself in solitude.

— Edgar Degas

Inwardness

It is with art as with love: How can a man of the world, with all his distractions, keep the inwardness which an artist must possess if he hopes to attain perfection? That inwardness which the spectator must share if he is to understand the work as the artist wishes and hopes. . . . Believe me, talents are like virtues; either you must love them for their own sake or renounce them altogether. And they are only recognized and rewarded when we have practiced them in secret, like a dangerous mystery.

— Johann Wolfgang von Goethe

Stillness

You need not leave your room. Remain sitting at your table and listen. You need not even listen, simply wait. You need not even wait, just learn to become quiet, and still, and solitary. The world will freely offer itself to you to be unmasked. It has no choice; it will roll in ecstasy at your feet.

— Franz Kafka

Waiting, not seeking

Who can wait quietly while the mud settles?
Who can remain still until the moment of action?
Observers of the Tao do not seek fulfillment.
Not seeking fulfillment, they are not swayed by desire
    for change.

— Lao Tsu

Tranquility

To live in a vast and proud tranquility; always beyond. . . . To
have, or not to have, one's emotions, one's For and Against,
according to choice; to lower oneself to them for hours; to *seat*
oneself on them as upon horses, and often as upon asses: — for
one must know how to make use of their stupidity as well as of
their fire. To conserve one's three hundred foregrounds; also
one's black spectacles: for there are circumstances when
nobody must look into our eyes, still less into our "motives."
And to choose for company that roguish and cheerful vice,
politeness. And to remain master of one's four virtues, courage,
insight, sympathy, and solitude. For solitude is a virtue with us,
as a sublime bent and bias to purity which divines that in the
contact of man and man — "in society" — it must be unavoid-
ably impure. All society makes one somehow, somewhere, or
sometime "commonplace."

> — Friedrich Nietzsche

Self-affirmation

I know I am august,
I do not trouble my spirit to vindicate itself or be
    understood,
I see that the elementary laws never apologize,
I reckon I behave no prouder than the level I plant my
    house by after all.

I exist as I am, that is enough,
If no other in the world be aware I sit content,
And if each and all be aware I sit content.

> — Walt Whitman

210

Creating artistic space

The artist must build a structure, not in the way of being of service to society, but in the way of discovering the dynamism of the interior.

To do that, to keep up with your responsibilities and your fitness and still nurture your creative aspect, you must put a hermetically sealed retort, so that there is no intrusion, around a certain number of hours each day — however many you can honestly afford — and that time must be inviolate. . . .

It's like doing your exercises: you set aside a time when you're going to exercise, and that is a holy time. With your art, you should do the same: give a certain number of hours a day to your art, and make it consistent. Then, whether you're writing [or painting] or not, sit there for those hours: it's a meditation on communication and expression, the two factors in the art work. What will happen, ideally, is that gradually — and it might not be this week or next or even this year — as your given responsibilities drop off, there will be an expansion of the time available to you for the practice of your art. The point I'm making is that your work — that is, your art — and your job must not contaminate each other.

— Joseph Campbell

The virtues of routine

Routine is a ground to stand on, a wall to retreat to; we cannot draw on our boots without bracing ourselves against it. Our health requires that we should recline on it from time to time. Our weakness wants it, but our strength uses it. Good for the body is the work of the body, good for the soul the work of the soul, and good for either the work of the other.

— Henry David Thoreau

Carrying the work forward

A man who feels the urge to produce finds, as he goes on living and working, such constant opposition and difficulty that he can seldom enjoy even the day when he does bring off something good. Moreover, he has always the itch to do better, so that what he has done never seems enough, indeed scarcely worth noticing; only later, when the results appear, when he can see how his comrades have taken up his own hopes, realized them, carried them further, only then can he feel himself a whole together with others, and so at last a real being with a real life.

— Johann Wolfgang von Goethe

PERSEVERANCE

Abandon security

The unfriendliness of society to his activity is difficult for the artist to accept. Yet this very hostility can act as a lever for true liberation. Freed from a false sense of security and community, the artist can abandon his plastic bank-book, just as he has abandoned other forms of security. Both the sense of community and of security depend on the familiar. Free of them, transcendental experiences become possible.

— Mark Rothko

Will original talent survive?

We are richer today in all that can be inherited, all tricks of the trade, for example, and all mechanical contrivances, but the inborn, original talent distinctive of the artist seems to grow rarer and rarer. And yet I would affirm that there is as much of it as ever, only it is a delicate plant and cannot now find the proper soil, climate and care.

— Johann Wolfgang von Goethe

Denial of our own possibilities

The claims of contemporary art cannot be ignored in any vital scheme of life. The art of today is that which really belongs to us: it is our own reflection. In condemning it we but condemn ourselves. We say that the present age possesses no art: — who is responsible for this? It is indeed a shame that despite all our rhapsodies about the ancients we pay so little attention to our own possibilities. Struggling artists, weary souls lingering in the shadow of cold disdain! In our self-centered century, what inspiration do we offer them? The past may well look with pity at the poverty of our civilization; the future will laugh at the barrenness of our art. We are destroying art in destroying the beautiful in life. . . .

— Kakuzo Okakura

Equanimity

But thou hast only the right to work, but none to the fruit thereof. Let not then the fruit of thy action be thy motive: nor yet be thou enamored of inaction.

Perform all thy actions with mind concentrated on the Divine, renouncing attachment and looking upon success and failure with an equal eye. Spirituality implies equanimity.

— The Bhagavad Gita

Rest and good company

What is indispensable to inspiration? Two things: sound sleep and the provocation of a good book or a companion.

I honor health as the first Muse.

— Ralph Waldo Emerson

Natural cycles

It is right and proper that man should reach a pinnacle and then descend again, this is no cause for complaint. But, of course, it is a bitter experience to live through. When Michelangelo was an old man, he drew himself sitting in a child's pushcart.

— Käthe Kollwitz

Know when to stop

Better stop short than fill to the brim.
Oversharpen the blade, and the edge will soon blunt.
Amass a store of gold and jade, and no one can protect it.
Claim wealth and titles, and disaster will follow.
Retire when the work is done.
This is the way of heaven.

— Lao Tsu

BALANCE

Perfect balance

Content with what comes to him without effort of his own, mounting above the pairs of opposites, free from envy, his mind balanced both in success and failure; though he acts, yet the consequences do not bind him.

— The Bhagavad Gita

The beauty of the night

This is thy hour O Soul, thy free flight into the wordless,
Away from books, away from art, the day erased, the
      lesson done,
The fully forth emerging, silent, gazing, pondering the
      themes thou lovest best,
Night, sleep, death and the stars.

— Walt Whitman

Bring life and the world into harmony

. . . What we cannot express by the art of thinking, by the art of science or philosophy or logic, we can and should express by the poetic, visual, or some other arts. It is for that reason that I consider morals and aesthetics as one and the same; for they cover only one impulse, one drive inherent in our consciousness — to bring our life and all our actions into a satisfactory relationship with the events of the world as our consciousness wants it to be, in harmony with our life and according to the laws of consciousness itself.

— Naum Gabo

Keeping beauty alive

Man surrenders so readily to the commonplace, his mind and his senses are so easily blunted, so quickly shut to supreme beauty that we must do all we can to keep the feeling for it alive. No one can do without beauty entirely; it is only because people have never learned to enjoy what is really good that they delight in what is flat and futile so long as it is new. One ought at least to hear a little melody every day, read a fine poem, see a good picture, and, if possible, make a few sensible remarks.

— Johann Wolfgang von Goethe

Art and worship

Painting and so-called religious experience are the same thing. It is a question of the perpetual motion of a right idea.

As I see it, painting and what is called religious experience are the same thing, and what we are all searching for is the understanding and realization of infinity — an idea which is complete, with no beginning, no end, and therefore giving to all things for all time.

— Ben Nicholson

In praise of practice

I am a dancer. I believe that we learn by practice. Whether it means to learn to dance by practicing dancing or to learn to live by practicing living, the principles are the same. In each it is the performance of a dedicated precise set of acts, physical or intellectual, from which come shape of achievement, a sense of one's being, a satisfaction of spirit. One becomes in some area an athlete of God.

To practice means to perform, in the face of all obstacles, some act of vision, of faith, of desire. Practice is a means of inviting the perfection desired.

— Martha Graham

DEVOTION

Sing your song

An artist has got to get acquainted with himself just as much as he can. This is what I call self-development, self-education. . . . Educating yourself is getting acquainted with yourself.

Find out what you really like if you can. Find out what is really important to you. Then sing your song. You will have something to sing about and your whole heart will be in the singing. . . .

— Robert Henri

Seek no reward

The just man does not seek for anything with his works, for those who seek something with their works are servants and hirelings, or those who work for a Why or a Wherefore. Therefore, if you would be conformed and transformed into justice do not aim at anything with your works and intend nothing in your mind in time or in eternity, neither reward nor blessedness, neither this nor that; for such works are all really dead. . . . Therefore, if you want . . . your works to live, you must be dead to all things and you must have become nothing. . . . Therefore go into your own ground and work there, and the works that you work there will all be living.

— Meister Eckhart

DEVOTION

The purity of joy and suffering

Joy and suffering are two equally precious gifts both of which must be savored to the full, each one in its purity, without trying to mix them. Through joy, the beauty of the world penetrates our soul. Through suffering it penetrates our body. . . .

— Simone Weil

Trust in God

Sacrifice again all the pettiness of social life to your art. O God above all things! For it is an eternal providence which directs omnisciently the good and evil fortunes of human men. . . . Tranquilly will I submit myself to all vicissitudes and place my sole confidence in Thy unalterable goodness, O God! My soul shall rejoice in Thy immutable servant. Be my rock, my light, forever my trust!

— Ludwig van Beethoven

And finally ...

An artist spends himself like the crayon in his hand, till he is all gone.

— Ralph Waldo Emerson

ACKNOWLEDGMENTS

The author wishes to express her gratitude to all the publishers who have kindly granted permission to quote from their publications. Every effort has been made to trace copyright holders of materials in this book. In a few instances, publishers did not respond in time for acknowledgment in this place. The author wishes to apologize to anyone whose rights may appear to have been overlooked and would be glad to be informed of anyone who has not been consulted.

Quotations from *The Divine Milieu* by Pierre Teilhard de Chardin. Copyright © 1957 by Editions du Seuill, Paris. English translation copyright © 1960 by Wm. Collins Sons & Co., London; and Harper & Row, Publishers, Inc., New York. Renewed © 1988 by Harper & Row Publishers, Inc. Reprinted by permission of HarperCollins Publishers, Inc.

Excerpts from *A Joseph Campbell Companion, Selected and Edited by Diane Osbon*. Copyright © 1991 by The Joseph Campbell Foundation. Reprinted by permission of HarperCollins Publishers, Inc.

From *Tao Te Ching* by Lao Tsu, trans. Gia-fu Feng and Jane English. Copyright © 1972 by Gia-fu Feng and Jane English. Reprinted by permission of Alfred A. Knopf, Inc.

From *Artists on Art* by Robert Goldwater and Marco Treves, editors and compilers. Copyright © 1945 by Pantheon Books, Inc. Copyright renewed 1973 by Robert Goldwater and Marco Treves. Reprinted by permission of Pantheon Books, a division of Random House, Inc.

From *Of Divers Arts* by Naum Gabo. Copyright © renewed 1962 by Princeton University Press. Reprinted by permission of Princeton University Press.

From *The Ideas of Le Corbusier*. Copyright © 1981 Fondation Le Corbusier. Reprinted by permission of George Braziller, Inc.

Quotations from *The Art Spirit* by Robert Henri. Copyright © 1923 J.B. Lippincott Company. Copyright renewed 1951 by Violet Organ. Introduction copyright 1930 by J.B. Lippincott Company. Copyright renewed 1958 by Forbes Watson. Reprinted by permission of HarperCollins Publishers, Inc.

From *The Diaries of Paul Klee 1898-1918* by Paul Klee, edited with an introduction by Felix Klee. English translation from the German, authorized by Felix Klee © 1964 by The Regents of the University of California, University of California Press, Berkeley and Los Angeles. Permission granted by the Regents of the University of California and the University of California Press.

From *Letters on Cézanne* by Rainer Maria Rilke, edited by Clara Rilke, translated by Joel Agee. Translation copyright © 1985 Fromm International Publishing Corporation, originally published as *Briefe ueber Cézanne* copyright © 1952, Insel Verlag, Frankfurt. Used by permission Fromm International Publishing Corp.

From *Zen in the Art of Archery* by Eugen Herrigel. Copyright© 1953 by Pantheon Books, Inc. Copyright renewed 1981 by Random House, Inc. Reprinted by permission of Pantheon Books, a division of Random House, Inc.

From *The New Art of Color: The Writings of Robert and Sonia Delaunay* by Robert and Sonia Delaunay. Edited and with an introduction by Arthur A. Cohen. Translated by David Shapiro and Arthur A. Cohen, 1978 The Viking Press. Used by permission of Viking Penguin, a division of Penguin Books USA, Inc.

From *Apollinaire on Art. (1902-1918)*. Edited by L.C. Breunig, translated by Susan Suleiman, Translation copyright © 1972 by The Viking Press, Inc. Used by permission of Viking Penguin, a division of Penguin Books USA Inc.

From *The Courage to Create* by Rollo May. First published as a Norton paperback in 1994. Copyright © by Rollo May. Used by permission of W.W. Norton & Company.

From *Christian & Oriental Philosophy of Art* by Ananda K. Coomaraswamy. Originally published in 1943 by Luzac & Co., Ltd., under the title *Why Exhibit Works of Art*. Used by permission Dover Publications, Inc.

From *Martha Graham—An Autobiography: Blood Memory*. Copyright © 1991 by Martha Graham. Published by Washington Square Press Publication of Pocket Books. Used by permission of Doubleday, a division of Bantam, Doubleday Dell Publishing Group, Inc.

From *Agnes Martin*, edited by Barbara Haskell. Published by Whitney Museum of American Art, 1992. Used by permission of Agnes Martin.

From *Concerning the Spiritual in Art* by Wassily Kandinsky. Translated with an introduction by M.T.H. Sadler. Copyright © 1977 by Dover Publications, Inc. Used by permission of Dover Publications, Inc.

From *Tàpies*. New York: Guggenheim Museum, 1995. "Communication and the Wall" by Antoni Tàpies. Translated by Mary Ann Newman. Used by permission Fundació Antoni Tàpies, Barcelona.

From *The Book of Tea* by Kakuzo Okakura. Edited and introduced by Everett F. Bleiler. Copyright © 1964 by Dover Publications, Inc. Used by permission Dover Publications, Inc.

From *The Blaue Reiter Almanac* by Wassily Kandinsky and Franz Marc, editors. Translated by Henning Falkenstein. Translation copyright © 1974 by Thames and Hudson, Ltd., London; *Der Blaue Reiter* Copyright © 1965 by R. Piper & Co., Verlag, Munchen. Used by permission of Viking Penguin, a division of Penguin Books USA, Inc.

From *The Poetics of the Form of Space, Light and the Infinite* by Irene Rice Pereira. Copyright © 1969 by I. Rice Pereira. Used by permission of André Zarre Gallery, agent of the estate of I. Rice Pereira.

From "The Nature of Beauty: Nature as Beauty" by Gilah Hirsch, part of the symposium "The Nature of Beauty in Contemporary Art," at the New York Open Center, 1995. Used by permission of Gilah Yelin Hirsch.

From *The Arts and Their Mission*, by Rudolph Steiner. Translated by Lisa D. Monges and Virginia Moore. Copyright © 1964 by Anthroposophic Press, Inc. Reprinted by permission of Anthroposophic Press.

BIBLIOGRAPHY

Apollinaire, Guillaume. *Apollinaire on Art: Essays and Reviews 1902–1918*. Edited by Le Roy C. Breunig, translated by Susan Suleiman. New York: The Viking Press, 1972.

Anderson, Emily, ed. *The Letters of Beethoven* (3 vols.) . London: Macmillan, 1961.

Ashton, Dore. *About Rothko*. New York, 1983.

———. *Noguchi: East and West*. University of California Press, 1992.

Augustine. *De Ordine*. Translated by Robert P. Russell. Cosmopolitan Science and Art Service Co., Inc.

Aurobindo, Sri. *Selections from Sri Aurobindo's Savriti*. High Falls, N.Y.: Matagiri Books, 1975.

Baron, Stanley with Jacques Damase. *Sonia Delaunay: The Life of an Artist*. New York: Harry N. Abrams, Inc. 1995.

Bellows, George. *The Paintings of George Bellows*. New York, 1929.

Bergson, Henri. *Matter and Memory*. Translated by N.M. Paul and and W.S. Palmer. New York: Zone Books, 1991.

Berry, Wendell. *Standing by Words*. San Francisco: North Point Press, 1983.

Bhagavad Gita, The. Translation by Shri Purohit Swami. London: Faber and Faber, 1978.

Bronowski, J. *Science and Human Values*. Pelikan, 1964.

Campbell, Joseph. *A Joseph Campbell Companion—Reflections on the Art of Living*. Selected and edited by Diane K. Osbon. New York: HarperCollins Publishers, 1991.

———. *The Hero with a Thousand Faces*. Princeton University Press, 1976.

Chirico, Giorgio de. "Mystery and Creation" *London Bulletin*. 1938.

Chuang Tsu. *Chuang Tsu—Inner Chapters*. Translated by Gia-fu Feng and Jane English. New York: Vintage Books Edition, 1974.

Coomaraswamy, Ananda K. *Christian and Oriental Philosophy of Art*. New York: Dover Publications, Inc., 1956.

———. *Coomaraswamy—Traditional Art and Symbolism*. Edited by Roger Lipsey. Princeton University Press, 1977.

———. *The Transformation of Nature in Art*. New York: Dover Publications, Inc., 1956.

Coughlan, Robert. *The World of Michelangelo*. Time–Life Books, Inc., 1966.

Critchlow, Keith. *Time Stands Still*. New York: St. Martin's Press, 1982.

Degand, Leon. "Matisse à Paris" *Les Lettres Françaises*. Oct. 6, 1945.

Delaunay, Robert and Sonia. *The New Art of Color: The Writings of Robert and Sonia Delaunay*. Edited and with an introduction by Arthur A. Cohen. Translated by David Shapiro and Arthur Cohen. New York: The Viking Press, 1978.

Eckhart, Meister Johannes. *Meister Eckhart*. Translation by Raymond B. Blakney. New York: Harper Torchbooks, 1941.

Einstein, Albert. *The World As I See It*. Philosophical Library, 1949.

Emerson, Ralph Waldo. *The Collected Works of Ralph Waldo Emerson*. Cambridge, Mass.: The Belknap Press of Harvard University, 1979.

———. *The Conduct of Life*. New York: AMS Press, 1979.

———. *The Journals and Miscellaneous Notebooks*. Cambridge, Mass.: The Belknap Press of Harvard University, 1969.

———. *The Topical Notebooks of Ralph Waldo* Emerson. Edited by Susan Sutton Smith. University of Missouri Press, 1990.

Ficino, Marsilio. *Commentary on Plato's Symposium*. Translated by Sears Reynolds Jayne. University of Missouri Press.

———. *The Letters of Marsilio* Ficino. Vol. I. London: Shepheard Walwyn,Ltd., 1975. Vol. II. London: Shepheard-Walwyn, Ltd., 1978.

Gabo, Naum. *Of Divers Arts.* The A.W. Mellon Lectures in the Fine Arts, National Gallery of Art, Washington, 1959. Bollingen Series XXXV: 8. Princeton, N.J.: Princeton University Press, 1962.

Gauguin, Paul. *The Intimate Journals of Paul Gauguin.* Translation by Van Wyck Brooks. New York: Liveright Publishing, 1936.

Geldard, Richard G. *The Travelers Key to Ancient Greece. A Guide to the Sacred Places of Ancient Greece.* New York: Alfred A. Knopf, 1989

Ghiselin, B. *The Creative Process.* New York: American Library, 1952.

Gibran, Kahlil. *Spiritual Sayings of Kahlil Gibran.* Edited by Anthony Rizcallah Ferris. New York: The Citadel Press,1962.

Giedion-Welcker, Carola. *Comtemporary Sculpture.* New York, 1955.

Goethe, Johann Wolfgang von. *Italian Journey.* San Francisco: North Point Press, 1982.

Goldwater, Robert, and Marco Treves. *Artists on Art: From the XIV to the XX Century.* New York: Pantheon Books, 1945.

Gowing, Lawrence. *Henri Matisse: Sixty-four Paintings.* New York: Museum of Modern Art, 1966.

Graetz, H.R. *The Symbolic Language of Vincent van Gogh.*New York: McGraw-Hill Book Co., Inc., 1963.

Graham, Martha. *Martha Graham—An Autobiography: Blood Memory.* New York: Washington Square Press, 1991.

Guiton, Jacques. *The Ideas of Le Corbusier on Architecture and Urban Planning.* Translation by Margaret Guiton. New York: George Braziller, 1981.

Hammacher, A.M. and Renilde. *Van Gogh.* London: Thames and Hudson, Ltd., 1958.

Haskell, Barbara. *Agnes Martin.* New York: Whitney Museum of American Art, 1992.

———. *Burgoyne Diller.* New York: Whitney Museum of American Art, 1990.

Hegel, G.W.F. *The Philosophy of Fine Art*. Translated by F.P.B. Osmaston. Gordon Press.

Henri, Robert. *The Art Spirit*. New York: Harper & Row, Publishers, 1984.

Herbert, Robert L. *Modern Artists on Art*. Englewood Cliffs, N.J.: Prentice-Hall, Inc., 1964.

Herrigel, Eugen. *Zen in the Art of Archery*. New York: Vintage Books, 1971.

Hirsch, Gilah Yelin. "The Nature of Beauty: Nature as Beauty." Symposium "The Nature of Beauty in Contemporary Art." New York Open Center, 1995 (unpublished).

Holzer, Burghild Nina. *A Walk Between Heaven and Earth*: A Personal Journal on Writing and the Creative Process. New York: Bell Tower, 1994.

Huntley, H.E. *The Divine Proportion — A Study in Mathematical Beauty*. New York: Dover Publications, Inc., 1970.

Hutchison. E. *How To Think Creatively*. New York: Abingdon-Cokesbury, 1949.

Hüttinger, Eduard. *Max Bill*. Zurich: abc editions, 1978.

Huxley, Aldous. *On Art and Artist*. Edited and introduced by Morris Philipson. New York: Harper & Brothers, 1960.

Jacks, Lawrence Pearsall. *The Education of the Whole Man*. University of London Press, Partway Reprints.

Jeffers, Robinson. *Roan Stallion, Tamar and Other Poems*. New York: Modern Library, 1935.

Jianou, Ionel. *Brancusi*. New York, 1963.

Joyce, James. *A Portrait of the Artist as a Young Man*. Penguin Books, 1976.

Kahn, Louis I. "Architecture: Silence & Light" *On the Future of Art*. New York: The Solomon R. Guggenheim Museum and Viking Press, 1970.

Kandinsky, Wassily. *Concerning the Spiritual in Art*. Translated by M. T. H. Sadler. New York: Dover Publications, Inc., 1977.

———. *Kandinsky: Complete Writings on Art*. Edited by Kenneth C. Lindsay and Peter Vergo. London: Faber and Faber, 1982.

——— and Franz Marc [editors and authors]. *The Blaue Reiter Almanac*. New York: The Viking Press, Inc., 1974.

Kant, Immanuel. *Critique of Judgment*. Translated by J.H. Bernard. Library of Classics, Halner Press.

Keeble, Brian. "Work and the Sacred". London: *Temenos* No. 9, 1988.

Klee, Paul. *Paul Klee on Modern* Art. Translated by Paul Findlay. London: Faber & Faber, Ltd., 1966.

———. *The Diaries of Paul Klee 1898-1918*. Edited by Felix Klee. Berkeley: University of California Press, 1964.

Krishnamurti, J. *The Flame of Attention*. San Francisco: Harper & Row, Publishers, 1984.

Kupka, Frantisk. *Frantisk Kupka 1871–1957: A Retrospective*. New York: The Solomon R. Guggenheim Foundation, 1975.

Lao Tsu. *Tao Te Ching*. Translation by Gai-fu Feng and Jane English. New York: Vintage Books, 1972.

Lawlor, Robert. *Sacred Geometry*. New York: Crossroad, 1982.

Leonardo da Vinci. *The Notebooks of Leonardo da Vinci*. Compiled and edited by Jean Paul Richter. New York: Dover Publications, Inc., 1970.

Lipsey, Roger. *An Art of Our Own:The Spiritual in Twentieth-Century Art*. Boston & Shaftesbury: Shambala, 1988.

MacIver, Loren. *Loren MacIver*. Exhibition catalog. New York: Terry Dintenfass Gallery, Inc., 1993.

Matisse, Henri. *Henri Matisse*. ed. Alfred H. Barr. New York: Museum of Modern Art, 1931.

———. *Ecrits et prosos sur l'art*. Edited by Dominique Fourcade. Translated by Roger Lipsey. Paris, 1972.

May, Rollo. *The Courage to Create*. New York: W.W. Norton & Company, 1975.

Milliken, William M. "White Flower by Georgia O'Keeffe." *Bulletin of the Cleveland Museum of Art*. 1937.

Mintz, Lisa Messinger. *Georgia O'Keeffe*. New York: Thames and Hudson, 1988.

Miró, Joan. "Je travaille comme un jardinier. Propos receuillis par Yvon Taillander." English translation by Joyce Reeves. *xxe Siècle*. 1959.

Modersohn-Becker, Paula. *Paula Modersohn-Becker—The Letters and Journals*. Edited by Günter Busch and Liselotte von Reinken. Edited and translated by Arthur S. Wensinger and Carole Clew Hoey. New York: Taplinger Publishing Co., 1983.

Mondrian, Piet. *The New Art—The New Life: The Collected Writings of Piet Mondrian*. Edited and translated by Harry Holtzman and Martin S. James. New York: Da Capo Press, 1993.

Mozart, Wolfgang Amadeus. *Letters of Wolfgang Amadeus Mozart*. Selected and edited by Hans Mersman. New York: Dover Publications, Inc., 1972.

Munch, Edvard. The journals of Edvard Munch in the Munch Museet Library, Oslo, as quoted in Ragna Stang, *Edvard Munch: The Man and the* Artist. Oslo: Aschehoug-Tanum, 1977.

Nagel, Otto. *Käthe Kollwitz*. Translated by Stella Humphries. Greenwich: New York Graphic Society, Ltd., 1971.

Nash, Steven A. *Ben Nicholson: Fifty Years of His Art*. Buffalo: Albright-Knox Art Gallery, 1978.

Needleman, Jacob. *The Heart of Philosophy*. New York: Bantam Books, 1984.

Neumann, Erich. "Art and Time." *Art and the Creative Unconscious*. translated by Ralph Manheim. Bollingen Series LXI. New York: Pantheon Books, 1959.

Nicholson, Ben. *Ben Nicholson*. Exhibition catalog. Basel: Galerie Beyeler, 1968.

Nicholson, Winifred. *Unkown Colour: Paintings, Letters, Writings by Winifred Nicholson*. An anthology compiled by Andrew Nicholson. London: Faber and Faber, Ltd., 1987.

Nietzsche, Friedrich. The Philosophy of Nietzsche. New York: The Modern Library. Random House, Inc.

Noguchi, Isamu. Unpublished interview, Venice, 1986. From the archive of the Isamu Noguchi Museum.

Novalis. *Novalis Werke*. Herausgegeben und kommentiert von Gerhard Schulz. Munich: Verlag C.H. Beck.

Okakura, Kakuzo. *The Book of Tea*. New York: Dover Publications, Inc., 1964.

O'Keeffe, Georgia. Letter to Jean Toomer dated January 10, 1934. Fisk University Library.

Ouspensky, P.D. *Tertium Organum*. New York: Vintage Books, 1970.

Parrot, Louis. "Picasso at Work." *Masses and Mainstream*, New York, 1948.

Pereira, Irene Rice. *The Poetics of the Form of Space, Light and the Infinite*. New York: I. Rice Pereira, 1969 [privately published.]

Picasso, Pablo. *Picasso*. New York: Museum of Modern Art, 1939.

——. *Picasso on Art: A Selection of Views*. Edited by Dore Ashton. New York: Da Capo Press, 1972.

Plato. *The Republic*. Translated by B. Jowett. New York: Vintage Books.

Plato. *Timaeus and Critias*. England: Penguin Books, Ltd., 1976.

Portable Greek Reader, The. Edited by W.H. Auden. New York: Viking Press, 1952.

Rilke, Rainer Maria. *Letters on Cézanne*. Edited by Clara Rilke. New York: Fromm International Publishing Corporation, 1985.

Roditi, Edouard. *Dialogues on Art*. Santa Barbara: Ross-Erikson, 1980.

Roles, Francis C. *Voyage of Discovery. Sayings and Teachings of Francis C. Roles*. New York: The Society for the Study of Human Being, 1992

Rothko, Mark. *Possibilities*. 1947.

——. Correspondence with Katherine Kuh in the Archives of the Art Institute, Chicago.

Rumi, Jalal'uddin. *Open Secret: Versions of Rumi.* Trans. by John Moyne and Coleman Barks. Putney, Vt.: Threshold Books, 1984.

Sappho. *Songs of Sappho, The.* Mount Vernon: Peter Pauper Press, Inc., 1966.

Schopenhauer, Arthur. *The World as Will and Idea.* Translated by R.E. Haldane and J. Kemp. AMS Press.

Scott, Marion M. *Beethoven.* Quoted by Marion M. Scott. London: J.M. Dent & Sons, 1934.

Segal, William. *The Structure of Man.* Brattleboro, Vermont: Green River Press/Stillgate Publishers, 1987.

Segantini, Giovanni. *Giovanni Segantini.* Einführung in Leben und Werk by Dora Lardelli. Glattbrugg, Switzerland: Beobachter AG, 1983.

Shaftesbury, Earl of (Anthony Ashley Cooper, 3rd Earl of Shaftesbury). *Characteristics.*

Shantanand Saraswati, H. H. *The Man Who Wanted to Meet God: Myths and Stories that Explain the Inexplicable.* New York: Bell Tower, 1996

Sherman, F.F. *Albert Pinkham Ryder.* New York, 1920.

Stieglitz, Alfred. "A Portrait—1918," published in MSS, 1922.

Steiner, Rudolf. *The Arts and Their Mission.* Translated by Lisa D. Monges and Virginia Moore. Spring Valley, N.Y.: The Anthroposophic Press, 1964, 1986.

Stone, I. *Dear Theo.: The Autobiography of Vincent Van Gogh.* New York: New American Library.

Tàpies, Antoni. "Communication on the Wall", translated by Mary Ann Newman. New York: Guggenheim Museum, 1995.

Teilhard de Chardin. *The Divine Milieu.* New York: Harper & Row, Publishers, 1968.

Ten Principal Upanishads, The, translated W.B. Yeats and Shri Purohit Swami. New York: Collier Books, 1975.

Thoreau, Henry David. *The Journal of Henry David Thoreau.* Edited by Bradford Torrey and Francis H. Allen. Salt Lake City: Gibs M. Smith, Inc., 1984.

————. *Thoreau on Man and Nature*. A compilation by Arthur G. Volkman. Mount Vernon: Peter Pauper Press, Inc., 1960.

Tobey, Mark. *Mark Tobey*. Translated by Margaret L. Kaplan. London: Thames and Hudson, 1966.

Tulku, Tarthang. *Gesture of Balance*. Emeryville, Calif.: Dharma Press, 1977.

Underhill, Evelyn. *Mysticism*. New York; Dutton, 1961

Vollard, Ambroise. *Paul Cézanne: His Life and Art*. New York, 1937.

Weil, Simone. *Waiting for God*. New York: Harper Colophon Books, 1973.

Whitman, Walt. *Leaves of Grass*. New York: Viking Press, 1959.

Wordsworth, William. *Selected Poems of William Wordsworth*. Edited by Solomon Francis Gingerich. Cambridge, Mass.: Houghton Mifflin Company, 1923.

Wright, Frank Lloyd. *An Autobiography*. New York: Horizon Press, 1932.

Wurman, R.S. "What will be has always been. The words of Louis I. Kahn," *The Invisible City*. International Design Conference at Aspen. New York: Access Press/Rizzoli, 1986.

Zarnescu, Constantin. *Aforismele çi textele lui Brancusi*. Craiova, 1980.

ADDITIONAL SOURCES

[In addition to the preceding bibliography, here is a list of books that the author has found both useful and practical in her work.]

Bamford, Christopher, ed. *Homage to Pythagoras: Redisovering Sacred Science.* Hudson, N.Y.: Lindisfarne Press, 1980.

Cameron, Julia. *The Artist's Way: A Spiritual Path to Higher Creativity.* New York: Jeremy P. Tarcher/Putnam, 1992.

Doczi, Gyorgy. *The Power of Limits.* Boulder, Co. and London: Shambhala, 1981.

Goldberg, Natalie. *Writing Down the Bones.* Boston: Shambhala Publications, 1986.

Needleman, Carla. *The Work of Craft.* New York: Kodansha America, Inc., 1993.

Samuels, M.D., Mike and Nancy Samuels. *Seeing with the Mind's Eye - The History, Techniques and Uses of Visualization.* New York: Random House, Inc., 1984.

Schneider, Michael S. *A Beginner's Guide to Constructing the Universe: The Mathematical Archetypes of Nature, Art, and Science.* New York: HarperCollins Publishers, Inc. 1994.

INDEX OF AUTHORS

Allard, Roger, 98
Apollinaire, Guillaume, 112, 121
Aquinas, Thomas, 33
Augustine, 148
Aurobindo, Sri, 37

Beethoven, Ludwig van, 4, 111, 220
Bellows, George, 94
Bergson, Henri, 15
Berry, Wendell, 7
Bhagavad-Gita, 101, 214, 216
Bill, Max, 137
Bissier, Julius, 97, 161
Blake, William, 103
Böhme, Jakob, 79, 85
Brancusi, Constantin, 110, 145, 166
Braque, Georges, 110
Bronowski, J., 167

Campbell, Joseph, 105, 208, 211
Cézanne, Paul, 174, 180
Chirico, Giorgi de, 29, 44
Chuang Tsu, 3, 205
Conrad, Joseph, 118

Coomaraswamy, Ananda K., 38, 87, 113, 140, 141, 149, 158, 160, 163, 171, 174, 176, 179, 195
Corot, Jean-Baptiste-Camille, 102

Degas, Edgar, 208
Dehner, Dorothy, 167, 188
Delaunay, Robert, 80, 142
Delaunay, Sonia, 145
De Mille, Agnes, 60
Diller, Burgoyne, 14

Eckhart, Meister, 178, 207, 219
Einstein, Albert, 22, 75
Emerson, Ralph Waldo, 2, 14, 15, 19, 23, 27, 28, 33, 54, 58, 67, 68, 72, 84, 88, 98, 100, 110, 123, 125, 127, 133, 135, 201, 202, 205, 215, 220
Ernst, Max, 18

Ficino, Marsilio, 6, 30, 34, 73, 186, 206
Flaubert, Gustave, 204

Fuller, Buckminster, 39

Gabo, Naum, 64, 67, 87, 91, 119, 121, 129, 217
Gauguin, Paul, 128, 184
Geldard, Richard, 160
Gibran, Kahlil, 36, 44, 46, 52, 141
Gleizes, Albert & Jean Metzinger, 72, 107, 111
Goethe, Johann Wolfgang von, 22, 23, 54, 70, 92, 128, 150, 203, 204, 209, 212, 213, 217
Graham, Martha, 59, 61, 100, 168, 173, 194, 218

Hegel, G. W. F., 37, 48, 50, 128, 134
Heidegger, Martin, 181
Henri, Robert, 7, 20, 51, 60, 68, 90, 99, 103, 106, 137, 144, 151, 173, 196, 197, 199, 201, 219
Hepworth, Barbara, 187, 189
Heraclitus, 17
Herrigel, Eugen, 8, 177, 179
Hirsch, Gilah Yelin, 44, 103, 126, 131, 135, 152
Holzer, Burghild Nina, 43, 78, 100, 189
Huntley, H.E., 38, 45, 136

Huxley, Aldous, 69, 130

Jacks, L.P., 92
Jeffers, Robinson, 39
Joyce, James, 52, 70, 158
Jung, C.G., 4, 15, 58

Kafka, Franz, 209
Kahn, Louis I., 18, 141
Kandinsky, Wassily, 28, 49, 86, 90, 96, 97, 112, 117, 129, 188, 190
Kant, Immanuel, 34, 48, 71
Karasz, Ilonka, 9
Keats, John, 182
Keeble, Brian, 198
Kepler, Johannes, 147
Klee, Paul, 5, 17, 42, 56, 153, 164, 166, 180, 194, 199
Kollwitz, Käthe, 215
Krishnamurti, J., 78, 178
Kupka, Frantisk, 104

Lao Tsu, 9, 175, 181, 185, 206, 209, 215
Lawlor, Robert, 147
Leonardo da Vinci, 16, 59, 101, 168, 183
Le Corbusier, 8, 71, 117, 150, 182, 185
Lipsey, Roger, 165
Lowell, Amy, 182

MacIver, Loren, 58
Macke, August, 55, 80, 140
Marc, Franz, 130
Marées, Hans Von, 176
Martin, Agnes, 35, 56, 68, 200
Matisse, Henri, 21, 96, 126,
    136, 143, 152, 162, 165,
    169, 171, 172, 184
May, Rollo, 55, 76, 191
Metzinger, Jean, and Albert
    Gleizes, 72, 107, 111
Michelangelo, 70, 202
Miró, Joan, 45, 183
Modersohn-Becker, Paula, 43,
    163, 174, 186
Mondrian, Piet, 19, 21, 74,
    96, 114, 118, 132, 134,
    144
Moore, Henry, 66, 200
Mozart, Wolfgang Amadeus,
    161
Munch, Edvard, 154
Mundaka-Upanishad, 2

Needleman, Jacob, 29, 69
Neumann, Erich, 86
Newman, Barnett, 89
Nicholson, Ben, 77, 78, 123,
    146, 154, 155, 168, 197,
    218
Nicholson, Winifred, 13, 66,
    115, 153, 170, 172

Nietzsche, Friedrich, 84, 102,
    210
Noguchi, Isamu, 93
Novalis, 12, 48, 51, 54, 99

Okakura, Kakuzo, 132, 137,
    214
O'Keeffe, Georgia, 61, 144,
    155, 196
Ouspensky, P.D., 94, 110

Pascal, Blaise, 13, 32, 75
Pereira, Irene Rice, 12, 16,
    26, 84, 146, 147
Picasso, Pablo, 74, 145, 149,
    200, 203
Plato, 3, 30, 35, 42, 70, 85,
    107, 141
Plotinus, 6, 12, 14, 33, 36, 39

Rasa'il, 146
Redon, Odilon, 184
Rilke, Rainer Maria, 99, 150,
    170, 172, 195, 203
Roles, Francis C., 5, 32,
    65
Rosenberg, Harold, 98
Rothko, Mark, 88, 97, 136,
    143, 151, 213
Rumi, Jalal'uddin, 198
Russell, Bertrand, 166
Ryder, Albert Pinkham, 105

Sand, George, 197
Sappho, 4, 204
Schönberg, Arnold, 119
Schopenhauer, Arthur, 57, 93,
    116, 122, 124, 148
Segal, William, 51
Segantini, Giovanni, 122
Shaftesbury, Third Earl of,
    140, 142
Shakespeare, William, 31, 53,
    76, 181, 186
Shantanand Saraswati, H. H.
    65, 77, 132, 201
Steiner, Rudolf, 37, 73, 88,
    89, 114, 117, 131, 133,
    152, 202
Stieglitz, Alfred, 47
Still, Clyfford, 102, 104

Tàpies, Antoni, 46, 116, 127
Taylor, Thomas, 148

Teilhard de Chardin, 17, 91, 159
Thoreau, Henry David, 6, 53,
    81, 113, 125, 175, 180,
    196, 198, 199, 207, 212
Tobey, Mark, 208
Tulku, Tarthang, 65

Underhill, Evelyn, 81
Upanishads, 2

van Gogh, Vincent, 29, 79,
    95, 99, 101, 106, 171,
    173, 187

Weil, Simone, 52, 56, 169,
    220
Whitman, Walt, 46, 210, 216
Wilde, Oscar, 22, 38, 92
Woolf, Virginia, 169
Wordsworth, William, 126
Wright, Frank Lloyd, 15

ARTWORK CREDITS

xvi ASTRID FITZGERALD
Urform VII, 1989.
Casein, 39 x 26"

10 BENIGNA CHILLA
Composition III, 1993.
Etching, 14 x 11"

24 ASTRID FITZGERALD
Quantum III, 1994.
Pastel, 36 x 30"

40 NACHUME MILLER
Mt. Fuji (State I), 1992.
Etching, 36 x 23"

62 CATHRYN ARCOMANO
Mirem, 1978.
Oil, 20 x 24"

82 KARL MEYER
Untitled, 1984.
Woodcut on beeswax on
canvas, 240 x 215cm

108 BERNARD MAISNER
The Rain Forest, 1991.
Oil, gold leaf on canvas,
62 x 56"

138 MARY ELLEN DOYLE
Urban Lines, 1994.
Watercolor and Lithopen-
cil on paper, 14 x 9"

156 DIXIE PALMER
PEASLEE
Karakoram, 1995.
Acrylic on canvas, 50 x 40"

192 CHRISTIAN PELTEN-
BURG=BRECHNEFF
Burning Tree Painting No. III.
1987/88.
Oil on canvas, 80 x 68"

PHOTO CREDITS

xvi, 24, 62, 138   Maggie Nimkin

ABOUT THE AUTHOR

Astrid Fitzgerald is an artist, designer, writer, and lover of ancient philosophy and the sacred sciences. She was born and educated in Switzerland and works in New York City. She has exhibited her work widely in both Europe and America. Her paintings and constructions are based on the Golden Mean proportions, and she also finds inspiration in the images from the far reaches of space and the concepts of quantum physics.

CPSIA information can be obtained at www.ICGtesting.com
Printed in the USA
BVOW012148290712

296504BV00001B/4/P